PLAYING POKER
WITH THE SAS

TOM GLEESON is a stand-up comic and has performed in every capital city in Australia, as well as London, Edinburgh, Montreal, New York, Los Angeles, Singapore and Jakarta. He was nominated for the Helpmann Award for Best Comedy Performer in 2007 for his sell-out show TOM ON, which he followed up with TOM-A-THON in 2008.

He is a regular on Channel Seven's *The Morning Show* and has also appeared on *Rove, Sunrise, Good News Week, Australia's Brainiest Radio Star, Stand Up Australia* and as the Australian Fast Bowler on *Skithouse*. Tom has also appeared in *The Melbourne International Comedy Festival Gala* and has been selected to perform in their *Roadshow* every year from 2001 to 2007.

Tom Gleeson now works in radio. His first show, *The Tom & Subby Show*, which he presented with Subby Valentine, was nominated for an Australian Commercial Radio Award. He currently does the breakfast show on Mix 101.1 Melbourne.

PLAYING POKER WITH THE SAS

A COMEDY TOUR OF IRAQ AND AFGHANISTAN

TOM GLEESON

NEW
SOUTH

A New South book

Published by
University of New South Wales Press Ltd
University of New South Wales
Sydney NSW 2052
AUSTRALIA
www.unswpress.com.au

© Tom Gleeson 2008
First published 2008

All photos © Tom Gleeson 2006

National Library of Australia
Cataloguing-in-Publication entry

Author: Gleeson, Tom.
Title: Playing poker with the SAS: a comedy tour of Iraq and Afghanistan/
Tom Gleeson.
ISBN: 978 1 921410 91 8 (pbk.)
Subjects: Gleeson, Tom – Anecdotes.
          Australia – Armed Forces – Middle East.
          Comedians – Australia.
          Stand-up comedy – Australia.
          Soldiers – Social life and customs – 21st century.
          Australian wit and humor.
Dewey Number: 792.230994

Design Josephine Pajor-Markus
Cover Sandra Krumins
Printer Ligare

This book is printed on paper using fibre supplied from plantation or
sustainably managed forests.

This book is dedicated to all Australian Defence personnel who are far away from home doing their job, whether they agree with why they are there or not.

CONTENTS

ACKNOWLEDGMENTS

Thanks to Phillipa McGuinness who found me and thought that my story was worth writing down and to my editors Sandra Davies and Chantal Gibbs who smoothed out my story to make me seem cleverer than I really am. Thanks also to my wife Ellie, who has heard every funny idea I've ever had, whether she has wanted to or not. Thanks to the Forces Entertainment Australia for taking me over there and, more importantly, returning me safely. And finally, a very big thanks to the RAAF band who, with a great sense of humour, set up and packed up the stage every night with not one complaint or minor grumble.

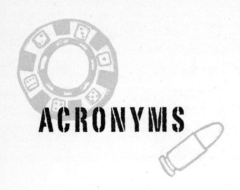

ACRONYMS

ADF   Australian Defence Force
ASLAV   Australian Light Armoured Vehicle
CBA   Combat Battle Armour
CBA   Commonwealth Bank of Australia
DFAC   Dining Facility
DMB   Death March for Bargains
GPS   Global Positioning System
HQ   Headquarters
HUAWP   Hurry Up and Wait Party
IED   Improvised Explosive Device
ISOPREP   Isolated Person Report
IZ   International Zone

MEAO	Middle Eastern Area of Operations
NATO	North Atlantic Treaty Organisation
OPSEC	Operational Security
PT	Physical Training
QT	Quiet
RAAF	Royal Australian Air Force
RPG	Rocket Propelled Grenade
SAS	Special Air Service
TCN	Third Country National
TLA	Three Letter Acronym
TLS	Taliban's Last Stand
WM	Wanking Machine
WMD	Weapon of Mass Deception

1

THE ASSIGNMENT
SEPTEMBER 2006

'Do you want to do some gigs in Baghdad?' my manager asks me on the phone. The answer is, yes. How could I refuse? Do you want to do a gig at The Comedy Store? Yeah, sure. Do you want to do Edinburgh again? Yeah, whatever. Do you want to perform in a war zone? *Fuck yeah!*

When you do stand-up there is always a perverse desire to perform in weird places. Up until this point, the weirdest gig I had ever done was on a helipad of a skyscraper in Jakarta, on a stage that was built from scratch by an over-abundant local labour force. But to perform for Australian troops during a war, that's a whole new adventure.

This is not why I got into comedy. I got into comedy because I was a kid with red hair and freckles and the only way I could get girls to like me was to make them laugh. When I was at uni I entered a stand-up competition and won. Well, after that I thought being a comedian was the best thing ever. It was like being in a band without having to carry any instruments. My whole career up to now had been about following my nose. When I started, I thought I'd keep doing this comedy thing until it got boring. Now, with a few gigs coming up in Baghdad, I know I won't be quitting any time soon.

'All right,' says my manager, 'I'll give your number to a guy from the army and he'll give you a call.'

Thanks, manager. You can have ten per cent of my earnings, but you won't get ten per cent of this experience.

FITZROY, MELBOURNE – 1 WEEK LATER

The call comes through from the army man, who tells me he can meet me anywhere I want. He's calling from Canberra, so I say, 'Meet me around the corner from my house in Melbourne.' *I'll be able to tell how serious he is by how far he's willing to travel.*

'What time?' *He's serious all right. No small talk from this guy.*

'Ten in the morning,' I answer. I always think that ten is an easy way to start the day and an easy appointment to keep.

When the day rolls around, I sleep in.

Okay, I am not proud of this, it just happened. The army man calls me on my mobile. 'Hello? I'm sorry. Did I wake you up?' he says.

Of all the people to sleep in for! This is an army man we're talking about. When he said ten o'clock, he meant TEN HUNDRED HOURS! So I use the oldest excuse in the book, 'Sorry, my voice is croaky 'cos I haven't spoken today yet.' Fortunately I get there in a flash because the walk from my bed to the café takes about one minute.

When I arrive I spot him straightaway. It's not because Mark is wearing a uniform, he's not, but everyone else in this hip inner city café is. Too funky hair, artistic tattoos, skinny black jeans, but there's Mark, a cuddly looking man dressed in clothes comfortable for Canberra. He is sitting at a table with a manila folder that contains a map of the Middle East tantalisingly sticking out.

I forget to ask Mark how he found me. I've heard that the army had been sneaking into gigs to find comedy acts. This was not something I had been actively seeking. Maybe they had already worked through a long list of comedians and I was the first one to say yes. Maybe they heard I had gone to boarding school and was used to sleeping in close quarters with people I didn't like and knew how to do a hospital corner. I like doing gigs. But I don't sit around thinking about how I got them.

It has been a long time since Kylie Minogue travelled up to entertain the diggers in East Timor, but there's nothing hip about boosting troop morale in an unjust war like Iraq. In the newspapers, there have been stories about how The Whitlams wouldn't go over, and Col Joye, who had performed for the Aussie troops in Vietnam, said he wouldn't go either. But Col forgot to mention that no one had asked him in the first place. The Australian Government obviously wants troop morale to go up, not down.

So I am quick to tell Mark that I do not support the war. In fact, prior to the 2003 Iraq invasion, I was at the peace march with tens of thousands of people jammed together down Swanston Street, Melbourne. It wasn't just the usual uni suspects either, there were people in suits alongside families with prams. It was the biggest peace march since the Vietnam War. Do you remember it? No one does. It's like it never happened.

'No problem,' Mark answers. 'A lot of soldiers don't think we should have invaded Iraq, either.' Ah-ha! The old doing-it-for-the-diggers argument. This doesn't solve the dilemma for me. It isn't the reason I'm interested in going. To be honest, I just want to go over and 'have a look'. I really don't think the course of the war is going to be changed by a tall, thin, red-headed comedian doing a few jokes for the troops. Later, when I tell my parents, family and friends about going over I find nothing but unanimous support. *It'll be an adventure! You'll get to travel and see the world!* These words of encouragement were a bit too World War I for my liking.

Mark doesn't seem too fussed about my motives for going, he's just happy that I want to. I start thinking that perhaps I was the only comedian he could find who was prepared to get shot for laughs. He shows me a few photos to give me an idea of what the performing conditions are like. He says that I will only be inside military bases, far behind enemy lines. It will almost feel like I'm on a holiday. Though I can't quite get over that a lot of people in the 'holiday' snaps he's showing me are 'relaxing' in their flak jackets.

Then we get down to serious business. Mark pulls out the map to show me where I will be doing my upcoming *tour de force*.

'We'll be going to a few bases in Iraq.' *Fair enough.* 'But first we'll be going here,' he points to a spot on the map. 'That's the supply base.' *I can handle that.* 'But you're not allowed to tell anyone you're going there.' *Huh?* 'Then we'll go to a few other countries that you're not allowed to tell anyone you're going to.' *R-i-g-ht.*

I ask him which ones. Even in a café full of lazy inner-city types Mark isn't prepared to disclose the names of these countries out loud. 'We'll be going here and here.' He points with his finger. 'These countries don't want anyone knowing they have a US military presence there. We have to honour that agreement.' Now, I'm no security expert but I would have thought that the best receptacle for military secrets was not a comedian – but there you go. Of course, this will later prove to be both unfounded and founded.

Mark gives me some forms to fill out, mainly for clothes measurements – among other things. I'll have to wear a uniform of King Gee work pants, shirt, Blundstone boots and a black windcheater with a big Australian flag on the arm. The idea here is to protect my own clothes with the added bonus that I'll look like a patriotic plumber who has taken a wrong turn and ended up in a war.

I also give Mark some details for getting my diplomatic passport. *This is now becoming like some totally James Bond shit!* But my favourite pencil-pushing form is called the ISOPREP (Isolated Person Report). It has to be filled out so that I can be identified if I get taken hostage. *These gigs are sounding better by the minute.* What I have to do is write down questions that only I can answer, like: What's my favourite colour? What was the name of my first dog? Where did I go on holidays as a kid? That sort of thing.

As Mark explains matter-of-factly, 'If you're taken hostage you'll have a bag on your head. The SAS will come kicking through the door. They'll be shooting people all around you while yelling out these questions. That's how they'll know that you are *you*.'

You know what, that's a bit too much pressure for me. When I'm doing my internet banking in the comfort – and quiet –

of my own home and I have to re-confirm some password, I can barely remember my mother's maiden name, let alone all this shit that I'm now writing down months before I leave, in a café, and after I have slept in!

A scenario immediately goes through my head. Knowing my luck, the SAS will come charging through the door ...

'What's your favourite colour?' they shout.

'Green!'

BANG! BANG! BANG! Hostage-takers are getting shot around me.

'What's the name of your first dog?' they demand.

I stumble ... shit ... 'Butch ... or was it Fluffy?'

BANG! And I get shot in the head for having a short attention span! Imagine if your last dying thought was, *I should have paid more attention!*

I am beginning to have more than just a few reservations about this gig, but nothing compares to how Ellie, my girlfriend, feels about the whole thing. She is the only person who says I shouldn't go. By going to Iraq and making the troops laugh she says I'm helping the government sanitise the war, even if it's just a tiny little bit, and for that reason she can't agree with my decision. I ask her if she also disagrees because she is worried that I may get killed. She replies flatly, 'No.'

Ellie never tells me that I can't go, but she doesn't encourage me either. Like in all great relationships, I ask Ellie for her opinion and then I do what I want anyway ...

2

THE REHEARSAL
FRIDAY, 1 DECEMBER 2006

I will not be going solo over there on this tour. Joining me are country music trio The McClymonts, who have won a few Golden Guitar awards at Tamworth; singer-songwriter Alan Caswell who penned the theme song for the 1980s Australian soap, *Prisoner*; and Adrian Ross, a didgeridoo player who performed at the opening ceremony of the 2000 Olympic Games in Sydney. Not exactly your 'A List', but then again beggars can't be choosers. The 'A List' doesn't turn up to entertain the troops in an unpopular war that has long fallen off the front pages of the national newspapers. As it turns out, I couldn't have toured with a lovelier and more inspiring bunch of artists.

Alan Caswell proves to be a very fine performer. He has a vocal range that can just as easily soar up high with vibrato as it can down low. He demonstrates this beautifully with his cover of 'House of the Rising Sun', but he's equally comfortable winning us over with his own creations, including 'On the Inside' from *Prisoner* that gets a run, of course. In hindsight, he was a great benefit to have on a tour such as this because his portly exterior and flushed red face were always around when your self-esteem needed a boost at a time of lost breath or fatigue. He was also there to exclaim, 'I need a drink' every time we entered yet another military base where alcohol was banned.

Adrian Ross is a beaming, warm, friendly blackfella who lives in Brisbane but grew up in Deniliquin in New South Wales. Throughout the tour, when he could, Adrian never took more than four steps without snapping a photo. In rehearsal, he plays the didge solo as well as with the band, creating an amazing sound-scape.

When I first meet Adrian he says, 'Where do you live?'

'Fitzroy, in Melbourne.'

'We've got a lot of our mob living there.'

I take a big ironic punt, 'Yeah, we've been trying to get rid of them for years.'

He looks at me for a second before collapsing into laughter. That's when I know we will be firm friends. Throughout the tour, Adrian always has the ability to cheer me up with the question, 'How's your *moom*?' *Moom* is a Koori word for 'bum'. It's a great question, because upon reflection your mood is very much dictated by the condition of your arse.

Now for the stars of this ramshackle show – the McClymonts. They are three sisters from Grafton in country New South Wales, not too far from where I grew up near Tambar Springs, which is near Gunnedah, which is near Tamworth, which is near Sydney. Brooke is the eldest at 24. She's a beautiful brunette who sings and plays guitar. She has the same silly sense of humour as me, so we hit it off straightaway. Brooke and I can pull faces at each other for an hour and be perfectly content.

Next is Sam, all of 22, she plays bass and sings too. Sam is a blonde who reverses the stereotype with her quiet intelligence, but all the guys still go gaga for her. She's the kind of woman who will never have to worry about carrying her luggage because a besotted man will always fall out of a tree to offer help.

The baby of the trio is Molly, at 19. As well as singing with the others, she plays the electric mandolin. This black-haired youngest member of the group is the straight shooter. She is also vague as all get-out, but somehow has the ability to come out with verbal sniper fire just as everyone falls silent. I learn about Molly's talent early on in the tour when we first arrive at an army base and are instructed on the use of soap dispensers. These dispensers, located inside the port-a-loos, contain alcohol which means you don't need hand towels. Molly immediately blurts out, 'Oh no! Alan will be licking his hands dry!' *This is her first trip overseas. Man, she is really going to enjoy the rest of her life!*

Now, before you get too concerned about these three innocent country girls being thrown into a war zone to entertain a platoon of sex-starved army men, I'll let you know that they will be travelling with their beautiful mother, Toni, the hairdresser. Toni's role is to keep these gals looking beautiful, as well as making sure that everyone else remains 'polite'.

Last, but certainly not least, there's the Royal Australian Air Force (RAAF) band. This isn't a brass marching band; it is an arse-kicking rock band, of about fifteen musicians in total, with a full horn section playing with military precision. I had no idea that you could be a fully paid member of the armed forces and have as your sole job playing electric guitar in a rock band, but it turns out to be the case. I learn that they're going over to be the backing band, as well as playing their own tunes. Out front they have both a male and female on vocals. There's Jerry, who joined the RAAF band after deciding he was sick of singing in covers bands and wanted a mortgage and a dental plan; and then there's Stephanie, the Jesus freak who has an amazing voice but still has to sing in army fatigues.

The members of the RAAF band are all trained to aim and shoot rifles. They are armed for the tour and had to practice in a shooting range for the trip. This makes them sound like they're very multi-talented, but don't forget these guys are really just music nerds. In a fire-fight they will fill you with as much confidence as a chess club that has just been slung a submachine gun and told to defend their favourite part of the library.

Filling out the tour is army officer Lieutenant Colonel Greg McCauley who is in charge of the tour, and Warrant Officer Andrew Kelly who is in charge of being second-in-charge and clean-shaven. Both these men have already travelled to all the locations we will be going to, so they're the only ones who know what we're really in for. Lieutenant Colonel Greg looks a little bit like a public servant in uniform. He's been living in Australia for a long time but still has an English accent that adds to his dry charm. Warrant Officer Andrew has the clear eyes of a career army man who has lived a life of good health. He's guarded, yet warm.

The first time we all get together is at a rehearsal. None of us knew each other before now, so I guess everyone's reactions are much the same as mine. There is a lot of excitement. We are all trying to work out how and why we have all come to be here. Who are these weird people? Why were we chosen? How do I fit in? We all know that we are about to embark on a memorable trip, certainly one that will haunt many dinner-party conversations for a while upon our return. We will all be asked the same inevitable question when people hear we have been to Iraq. *What was it like?* But right now, it is the calm before the storm.

It is hard to work out why the other performers want to go to the Middle East. Entertainers are frivolous at the best of times so most of the day is spent sharing a laugh and putting faces to names. Most, like me, seem to be going for the adventure. No one seems to be overtly pro-war but then again, who is? Everyone is holding their cards pretty close to their chest though, because no one wants to get Lieutenant Colonel Greg or Warrant Officer Andrew off-side.

The rehearsal is mainly for the musicians. Everyone gets together and has a jam, though there may be a bit of sizing one another up as the artists play their respective set lists. I am blown away by everyone's musical ability, which leaves me in a bit of a quandary. I'm a comedian. For me, rehearsal involves saying, 'See that microphone. When I talk into it, I will make people laugh.' I am definitely the dark horse. No one knows what I'm going to do.

'I suppose you don't really need to rehearse your set do you, Tom?' asks Warrant Officer Andrew.

'Nope! As long as everyone can see me and hear me I'll be good to go,' I reply.

'And what are you planning on doing?' prods Greg.

'Bit of this, bit of that.' It's good to keep them guessing, and I don't feel eager to please. The way I see it, they need me more than I need them. Besides, I don't know what material I'm going to do tomorrow night, let alone in a couple of weeks.

3

THE DEPARTURE
TUESDAY, 19 DECEMBER 2006

Under no circumstances am I allowed to tell anyone the actual date I am leaving. It is a security risk. The Australian Defence Force (ADF) is obviously worried that there may be a terrorist who wants to make a name for himself by taking a slightly famous comedian hostage to further their cause. All I am permitted to tell my family and loved ones is that I'll be away over the Christmas and New Year period.

I know I'm going to miss everyone, especially Ellie, but when I weigh it all up Baghdad is probably going to be less stressful than Myer during the Christmas rush.

I also know that the trip will be alcohol-free, so I'm excited about the fringe benefit of detoxing over the Christmas break while everyone back home will be retoxing.

The departure day draws closer, and the more people ask me *Are you looking forward to going to Iraq?,* the more I start to think that I may have made a mistake. At school I always felt sorry for the conscripts who died in the Vietnam War, because they didn't have a choice. I know it's not quite right but I always thought that the volunteers who died in Vietnam were a little foolish because they had chosen their destiny. And somehow, here I am having volunteered to go to a war zone where I will have to face my worst fear: finding myself in a dangerous situation because of my own free will.

My brain can't process that I will actually be in Iraq soon, a place that looks so unwelcoming in the news. I can't picture myself being there. I can't even imagine getting there, so I opt for just putting one foot in front of the other and seeing what happens.

Just before I leave this sunburnt country, I am required to have a comprehensive health check by an army-approved doctor. As it turns out I am in perfect condition to go and get shot. The only thing I have to endure are some vaccinations. A few of these are double and triple bungers that inoculate me against several long-forgotten diseases at once. I am the only one of my friends who is now immune to the Black Death.

But the one that caps it off for me is being told that I need to take an antibiotic to ward against malaria. The only side effect is that my skin will be more sensitive to sunlight. *Excuse me?* I've got red hair and fair skin and I'm about to go into the desert and I'm taking a drug that makes me MORE sensitive to sunlight. That's like swapping my SPF 30+ for an SPF 4 without me knowing, and then telling me that instead of wearing a hat I should wear a giant magnifying glass on my bald head. And malaria? I thought I was going into the desert during winter, what are mozzies doing over there? Someone is taking the piss. I thought that was my job.

On the day of departure I'm feeling a bit nervous, more with anticipation than fear. I have complete faith that the Australian Army will look after me. Besides, I know it's not good PR for the army to lose a comedian on their trip, because it will be really difficult to get more entertainers to volunteer after that.

Ellie drops me off at Melbourne Airport, a trip we've made many times before. I've been with Ellie for my entire professional life as a comedian, so she's used to dropping me off here and not seeing me for months at a time – but this time it's different. There is a genuine sense of danger and she doesn't even know where I'm going. Then again I don't know where I'm going. I know I'll be departing Australia from Sydney Airport in the next 24 hours, but I'm still not exactly sure when.

Ellie hugs me a little bit too tightly. 'Look after yourself,' she says.

I don't know what that will involve, but I say, 'Sure'.

I am reunited in Sydney with my new-found performing buddies – Adrian the didge player, Alan the folky, the McClymont girls and the RAAF band. We are all set to go with identical army-issued khaki luggage. Now our bags not only all look the same but if they were dumped in long grass over there we would never find them again. So in a brief moment of clarity – and practicality – I bring out my Gleeson-issued texta and put a big 'TG' onto my bag. There's nothing worse than losing your luggage in a war zone. It is one thing to be in Baghdad, but without a toothbrush? No thanks.

Our scheduled flight isn't on the departure board. *O-k-a-y.* *I get the feeling this whole trip is going to be off the record.* We are flying with a private aviation company that specialises in transporting the military. I'm relieved to hear that we'll be travelling on a big Boeing 747 and it will be like any other regular flight except there won't be a drinks trolley. There's also very little chance of anyone hijacking the plane, given that every second chair is fitted out with a plain-clothed, fully trained specimen of the Australian Defence Force. We'll be sharing the plane with soldiers who are fighting a war I have the luxury of not agreeing with. *Interesting bedfellows.*

I fear I may have already created a rift because I run straight through customs and enter the Qantas Club (and we're not even flying Qantas). I sweet-talk my way in so that I can relieve the unease with a beer and use the complimentary internet facilities. I figure I should start blogging on MySpace in case it's the last people hear of me. I can't tell my other travelling companions where I am because we don't have our mobile phones with us. I decide to try not to look too smug when I get on the plane to avoid getting picked on for affording myself a last bit of luxury.

Just before we board we have to go to the airport media room so that some of the acts can do some interviews.

I decline because I prefer to do my media when I come back home and am free from the watchful eye of the army PR guy. As we enter the room, coming the other way is none other than Prime Minister John Howard. *Remember him?*

The army PR guy can't resist. 'Mr Howard, I'd like to introduce you to these wonderful Australians who are going over to the Middle East to entertain our troops!' Howard swivels on his heel and is quick to say hello. No cameras. No press. Just him and us. Now, I am not a fan of his work, so I'm in a conundrum. How do you say hello to a man you don't like?

First, let me set the scene. He is short. I am tall, but he is *very* short. Also, his right hand is quite crooked. It comes at me for a handshake at a weird angle that makes me think, *Do I have to touch it? Is there some way out of this?* He wears a hearing aid in both ears; I find this alarming because this has never been publicised. I imagine the government thinks it makes him look too old and 'unelectable'. As it turns out, hearing aids are the least of his problems. I just can't believe that the prime minister of our country can't hear properly. The thought of it casts me back to all those hours of footage where I had seen people yelling at him during question time and he's just sitting there copping the abuse. He must have had his hearing aids switched off! His wife Janette is here too and I forget to talk to her, which kills me afterwards because for over 11 years we have never heard her speak. I should have made her say hello. I imagine that her voice would be either embarrassingly high or embarrassingly low.

When John Howard shakes my hand with his weird crooked talon he says, 'I just want to say thank you for going over there to cheer up our troops.'

'That's all right. I wouldn't be able to do it if you hadn't depressed them in the first place.' *Well, that's what I wish I said.* In reality, I just smile from behind my sunglasses and nonchalantly reply, 'You're welcome'. I can't quite bring myself to ruin an old man's day.

So this is how people go to war these days. No streamers flying towards steamships on docks with beautiful wives and girlfriends waving goodbye. No brass bands, not even any uniforms. When Australians go to war now they walk through the duty free at Sydney Airport. The only thing that gives them away is that you normally don't see large numbers of men hanging out together who look *that* healthy and *that* well-shaven.

The flight is a long one. First to Darwin, then off to the middle of the Indian Ocean to an island with an airstrip, and then off to war. There is a level of intensity painted on the faces of soldiers that rubs off on all us performers. We don't really know what we're in for, but some of the soldiers have already been there. I feel too shy to talk to any of them because they look like they are a million miles away. Maybe they're thinking about the families they've left behind. Maybe they're thinking about what they've got ahead of them. Maybe the conflicting thoughts of both.

During the flight, while everyone's asleep, I go and chat to the flight attendants. 'What's it like working on these flights?' I ask.

'Great!' They tell me. 'All the soldiers are really polite and there's never any trouble because no one is allowed to drink. It's on the way home that they let their hair down.' *Well, only as much as you can let short-back-and-sides down.*

During a stopover I ask a friendly-looking chap in his early twenties what he'll be doing over there. 'I'm going to be driving trucks over in [one of the countries we can't mention] ...' he tells me. 'I've done it before. Six months' worth. It's a pretty easy job and it pays a lot better than driving trucks back in Australia. I've been looking forward to it.'

This sets the tone of the trip for me. It seems people in the army actually can't wait to get over there. I suppose when you do all this training and then finally get a chance to use all of your skills, you take it. I always thought that no one would want to go into combat. But that would be like me dreaming up all these funny ideas and then not performing them on stage. *Then again, in my job when I die, it's only a metaphor.*

4

SECRET COUNTRY NO. 1
WEDNESDAY, 20 DECEMBER 2006

It's a cold morning when we land in an airstrip in the middle of nowhere in the first country I cannot name. We're all feeling ratshit but there's no Qantas Club here to solve our problems. We disembark the 747 down a stairway straight onto the tarmac. Our bags get unloaded onto a forklift pallet. We'll see them again later, I presume. All the musicians show a passing concern for their instruments but mostly we're all just taking it in. All we can see is tarmac, empty army containers, a couple of tent shelters flapping in the breeze, a couple of port-a-loos and desert. *Is this what it's going to be like?*

Many of the army people take the chance to immediately light up a cigarette. There's an unusually large number of smokers, but I suppose your fear of lung cancer is significantly diminished when you have a genuine chance of getting shot.

It seems that this is not what it's going to be like, as we soon take off in a minibus — it's actually the same model that I used to go to primary school in. We're all cracking jokes amid our jet lag when suddenly it catches our eye. There it is. Sitting next to the driver is a gun — a big one. You see guns all the time in movies, but there's nothing more menacing, that leaves you so completely vulnerable, than seeing a semiautomatic rifle that may have been used or is about to be used to kill someone.

I have to ask the driver, 'What do you need the gun for?'

'Just in case,' comes the reply.

We're not even in Iraq yet and already there are 'just in case' scenarios. The soldier who is driving also has an iPod — just in case.

'Just in case I get bored!' he adds. We all laugh — probably a bit too much. We're starting to have a genuinely good time, but I can't help thinking that we're laughing so much that it is like that scene you see in movies where everyone is carefree and having a great time just before things go horribly wrong. Luckily, there is no big dose of reality. Not yet, anyway.

The airbase in Secret Country No. 1 is where the majority of the coalition supplies arrive on their way to Iraq and through to Afghanistan. My first view of the base is of some giant concrete bunkers with their enormous roofs caved in. The driver takes great pleasure in telling us that the French built these 'impenetrable' concrete hangars for the country. During Gulf War I, after the Iraqis invaded, they removed the country's planes and placed their planes in the hangars instead. The United States promptly put a hole in the roof of every hangar with their missiles. Not one hangar was untouched. I've seen a lot of World War II relics at the War Memorial, but Gulf War I relics? There's something eerie about witnessing the aftermath of a relatively recent war. It's almost as if it hasn't become history yet because it hasn't been taught in high schools. The damage to these enormous structures can't help but remind you that a lot of people died here. Subsequently, Secret Country No. 1 has sued France for their faulty engineering. The case is yet to be resolved.

When we finally arrive at our destination, we discover

that the Australians have a base within the base. It is a *little* slice of Australia that is inside a *giant* slice of America that is inside a *massive* slice of this country I cannot name.

The main recreation building is made of corrugated iron and inside is a kitchen with a bar that serves non-alcoholic 'near beers'. A few soldiers relax while watching Australian television via satellite. The accommodation is a series of demountable buildings neatly laid out with bunks for about eight people in each. They look like the kind of buildings you'd find on a construction site, though they look a bit more permanent here against the backdrop of the barren dusty landscape.

The 50 or so Australians here are in charge of sending all the supplies and equipment through to the rest of the Middle Eastern Area of Operations (MEAO). And the only thing that really makes the Australian area different from the rest of the base is that it has Australians in it and an Australian flag. The Americans aren't allowed to enter uninvited, and every now and then the Aussies have a barbecue with hotdogs because sausages aren't available.

We are given an itinerary: have a little bit of lunch, have a little look around, have a little bit of dinner, then do a show. *No mucking about! Straight into it.*

When you travel into a war zone, even lunch is an experience. Lunch is always at the DFAC – short for dining facility. You walk in and there's a drum full of sand that you 'clear' your weapon into. 'Clearing' involves firing the gun into the sand to make sure you have no bullets left in the chamber. You don't want a bullet in your burger. I haven't been issued with a gun yet so I don't need to worry about this. *When are they going to give me a gun? I think I'll ask tomorrow.* Before you can set foot inside the DFAC you have to sign in and write down the time you enter, just like an RSL. I can't resist, so I sign in as Don Bradman at 99:94 hours.

The supervising US soldier says, 'Mr Bradman, I think you've made a mistake with your time.' I change it, hoping that some other Australian will see it and have a giggle when they sign in later.

The DFAC is huge. It's like a university cafeteria squared. It would have to be to feed both the American and Australian contingent here. Throw away the vision of that long-gone mess tent of the 4077 where the echo of Hawkeye's complaints about army food faintly lingers – here, it is incredible. The DFAC is run by the Americans, the Australians are just guests. There is an amazing array of food: a carvery with delectable roasted meats, baked vegetables, an overload of condiments, a sea of bain-maries filled with pastas, stir-fries, salads, a seemingly unlimited supply of soft drinks and, wait for it, Baskin-Robbins ice-cream for dessert.

Soldiers here look a bit overweight, which doesn't surprise me. I figure if they get too fat it's no big deal, they can always go and burn off those excess kilos at one of the gyms. That's right. There are gyms to work off the junk food you eat in a war zone. In fact, the camps are kitted out with recreational buildings complete with the latest Xbox gaming consoles. After a hard day at the office shooting people you can go back, relax, get on the Xbox and unwind by shooting people.

It's at the DFAC that I have my first interaction with a character from the endlessly fascinating US military contingent. Brian, who's wearing a grey tracksuit since he's just finished training at the gym, sits next to me because I 'look out of place'. He's older than I am, late thirties, maybe older, but a damn size fitter than I was at 20. He has silver hair fashioned to a very close-cropped flat top. He asks me what I am doing here and I tell him.

'I'd just like to say thank you on behalf of America for coming over here to entertain the troops,' he says.

'I'm not here to entertain you. I'm here to entertain Australians, but you're most welcome to come along to the show tonight if you want.'

Brian seems to find my plain-speaking ways funny. After fielding the requisite questions about what it's like to be a comedian – How did you start? At uni. Are you funny all the time? *No.* Have you ever died on stage? *Yes.* Where's the weirdest place you've done a gig? *Here.* – I turn the focus on him. What was he doing here? Brian tells me he works in security looking after diplomats.

'Do you have to wear a flak jacket?' I ask.

'No. The jobs I do are more like in-out, with a .45 in the gym shorts. Good luck with the show tonight, and once again we really appreciate you coming over here.' With that he was off. Why don't we see guys like Brian on the news and what does 'in-out with a .45 in the gym shorts' *actually* mean? *Like I said, fascinating.*

I was more interested in Brian than he was in me and he knew this. As an entertainer I'm dime-a-dozen for the Americans. Last week, they had some heavy metal bands come through and next week they'll be entertained by the Dallas Cowboys' cheerleaders. Maybe Brian will come to our little Australian show. Maybe not.

Later on, Warrant Officer Andrew allows me to dawdle around the camp. I'm getting a bit of perspective, while dodging military vehicles, when I come across a café called 'Green Beans'. Believe it or not it's an American franchise that only has outlets in war zones. So just because I can, I grab a doughnut and a latte, even though I'm still chock-full of dinner. It costs just a few US dollars. I get handed the change, but instead of coins they have tokens made out of cardboard. I'm not sure if this is for security reasons or simply convenience. I suppose the military doesn't need any more tiny pieces of metal whizzing around the place than they have already.

Green Beans is propped up conveniently next to a McDonald's, a Subway and a Pizza Hut. What would the diggers of Gallipoli or the Kokoda trail make of this? There is no fly-blown bully beef or rock-hard biscuit here.

There is a tourist shop too where you can buy badges and caps in support of Operation Iraqi Freedom. *Is that what they call it?* It's here that I first meet what's known in the army as TCNs – Third Country Nationals. These people are flown in, mainly from India and Pakistan, to do the menial tasks around the camp like laundry, cooking and running the tourist shops. You see, they can't have locals working in the camp because they pose a security threat. Hearts and minds are clearly a long way from being won over, I thought. After buying a desert camouflage version of the Australian Flag badge, I have a little bit of a chat about cricket and then go on my way.

The RAAF band is truly remarkable. These poor bastards not only have to play on stage for the whole two-hour show, they also have to set up and break down the entire stage rig. Every night. The military don't do things by halves. Our stage set-up would have made a lot of clubs back in Australia embarrassed about their equipment.

To be honest, the first night is a bit of a blur. Thanks to the jetlag I have been awake for close to 20 hours. That first night, I remember Adrian's didgeridoo silencing the crowd of about 200 soldiers – it's a sound that instantly connects any Australian with home. Alan, who is a polished performer, has the crowd singing along to his version of 'House of the Rising Sun'. Then the band takes a break and I am on.

No one on our tour has seen me perform before now, so I don't want to disappoint. I can barely stand I'm so dizzy with fatigue. I remind myself that my fatigue doesn't even compare to that of a soldier who has done a real day's work. Long before I left for this tour I decided I wasn't going to pussyfoot around. I realised that these soldiers have put their lives on the line, so nothing I was going to say now is going to offend them. If they were anything like the Victorian Police, whom I had performed for previously, they would have a black sense of humour. So I go hard.

'Are there any Australians in?' I yell. *Huge cheer.*

'Are there any Americans in?' *Big cheer.* They love to let people know they are in the house.

'To you, I just want to say thank you for supporting Australia's war in Iraq.' Too much laughter comes from the Australians towards the Americans. Not so much laughter comes from the Americans. I feel the most alive I've felt on stage for a long time. Here I am in a war zone actually cheering up people who need it, not just supplying a few cheap laughs at a comedy club for blokes on a bucks' night. It is magic. I think I want to push this further.

'Are there any TCNs in?' My question is met by a deafening silence. 'Of course they're not here. That's because they're too busy cleaning up your shit for two dollars a day!' The place explodes. *This is going to be a fun night*. The McClymonts haven't even come out yet. They are going to melt everyone's hearts with their warm harmonies and country charm.

After the show, I ask Lieutenant Colonel Greg how long I was on stage for. 'About 25 minutes,' he tells me. I must have been enjoying myself, I was only meant to do 15. By now, I am barely standing. In the midst of congratulating me on what a good gig it was, people tell me, 'You look buggered!'

When I finally climb into my bunk I sink into a well-earned deep sleep.

If there's one thing that Americans have their head around it is breakfast. Maple syrup with flapjacks? *Why not.* French toast? *Yes please.* Molly McClymont and I start to worry that we are going to return to Australia a bit too chubby. For some reason, we are sure that we're going to get fat necks.

After breakfast, we have to go to the Australian store to get kitted up for the rest of the tour. In charge of the storeroom is a guy with the nickname of Lurch, notably for his extremely lanky stature. My head comes up to below his shoulder and I'm six foot five! He's the kind of guy people back home would point at in the street, but here he fits right in. We are given khaki winter snow gear for Afghanistan. *How cold is this tour going to get?* We are also given sleeping bags and flak jackets. The flak jackets are known as Combat Body Armour or CBA. The army loves a TLA (three-letter acronym). The jackets weigh about 15 kilos and have high-tech ceramic plates in the front and back.

'Do we need this because we're going to get shot at?' I ask.

'No one is going to shoot at you,' Lurch assures me.

'Well, then, I won't need the body armour,' I say cheekily.

'No, you will need it just in case.'

'Just in case – what?' I prod.

'Nothing.'

'Good, well I won't need it then.'

'You just need it. *Okay*?' Lurch insists. We're also given a helmet. Maybe we are going to ride a bicycle later? We then get handed sunglasses that are capable of keeping shrapnel out of our eyes – again 'just in case'. Now, I don't mind putting on sunblock 'just in case', but shrapnel-proof sunglasses are another matter entirely. *Just where are we going?*

5

IRAQ
THURSDAY, 21 DECEMBER 2006

When you wake up in a new country, that's when you feel like you've actually arrived. In this case though, just when we get settled, we have to leave. No sooner do we feel like unpacking than we have to return to the airbase. When we get to the airfield I take a little closer look at the faulty French engineering of those hangars. The concrete on the hangars is thick, the holes are huge. People have definitely died here.

The RAAF has two Hercules planes operating in the Middle East. Over the course of the tour we get to know the Hercules crews as they ferry us around the MEAO like normal passengers on a domestic flight. Flying in a Hercules is like taking a standard domestic flight, except that you have to check yourself in as luggage and get thrown in the hold. We sit on fold-down seats facing each other with body armour and helmets on and in the middle is a big pallet holding all our equipment.

The aircraft is loud. Especially when all four propellers are going. It gets so noisy that we need to wear earplugs. There's no way you can chat to the person next to you, so to pass the time I read *Flags of Our Fathers*, a book about the battle for Iwo Jima. There's nothing like reading about a past war to take your mind off the current one you're in. Once we're airborne they tell us we can take off our body armour because 'we're too high for anyone to get us'. *That's reassuring.*

We're up in the air for about an hour when the plane levels out and I get sent for. The pilot, who had seen the show last night, invites me up into the cockpit. I feel like a little boy who, for his birthday, has been escorted up to meet the Qantas pilot. It's beautiful up there, the sky is so clear. The plane is on autopilot. The pilot then gives me a set of headphones with a mic and explains that I can talk to the entire crew. I have a chat to someone in the tail of the plane who had previously seen me perform at a show in Bathurst. *One of the stranger ways of chatting to a fan.*

The pilot asks me what it is like being a comedian: *How did you start? Are you funny all the time? Blah blah blah …* I turn the focus around and ask him about flying. He tells me that when we go in for the landing we will either go in long and flat or really steep. Both of these approaches apparently minimise the risk of being hit by a Rocket Propelled Grenade (RPG), which I agree is a top idea. Going in long and flat means that 'the enemy' on the ground has no time to set its rocket site because the plane flies over too quickly. Going in steep means that the plane creates a smaller target area for the enemy, and is equally effective. Either way, all this talk of minimising risk is starting to sound *risky*. I look at the GPS as we cross the border into Iraq and suddenly I have this sinking feeling. *I cannot get out of this. I can't change my mind now. I am definitely going to Iraq.*

Later, if people were to ask me if I was scared over here, I could honestly say that this is one of only a few moments when I was. As a comedian I have travelled throughout Australia and all around the world many times over. The security staff at Melbourne airport now know me by name. I have flown way more than probability suggests I should live through, so I'm not a good flyer anyway. Now, here I am in a military aircraft flying into a war zone. I feel fairly confident until I hear this exchange through my headphones. The crew all know I can hear what is being said, which makes it worse.

My fan in the tail asks, 'Why are we flying on *this* side of the river?'

'What's wrong with that?' replies the pilot.

'It's just that I would be a lot more *comfortable* if we moved to the other side of the river.'

'Why?' the pilot pushes.

'Well, it was on *this* side of the river that there was *trouble*.'

Without a word spoken the pilot banks the plane heavily to the left and we move. There are no knowing looks. No winks at me to suggest everything will be all right. Just an uncomfortable silence in which my imagination, my own worst enemy, could run wild.

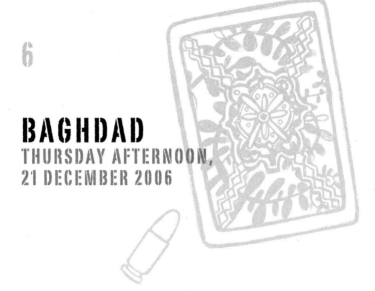

6

BAGHDAD
THURSDAY AFTERNOON,
21 DECEMBER 2006

Baghdad looks beautiful from a distance. It's the only way I would ever see this amazing city – certainly in the near future anyway. I am destined to spend my whole time here inside the Green Zone, a giant, heavily secured area where the US military and tiny Australian attachments reside. When we come in to land at Baghdad International Airport the pilot decides to take the steep trajectory. In we go. I look out the front of the plane and see the horizon. Suddenly, when we go in to land, the horizon simply fucks off – straight up. Then, out of the front of the cockpit my entire field of view is tarmac; and before I can blink twice we land with a huge skid. The landing is so abrupt I think we roll along the runway for just one metre.

We are deep inside the Green Zone so we can take off our flak jackets. *I never thought I would say this but, thank god. We are in Baghdad. We can relax now.*

The Green Zone is massive with three huge bases including Camp Victory, inside of which is the Australian corner. The Australians in Baghdad are in charge of providing security for the Australian Government and its ambassadors. There are about 60 army personnel there, as I understand, and they live among a few more Americans than that.

Here's a tip for you. If ever you get driven around a military facility in a war zone make sure you travel with the women. You get better service. I jump in the same car as the McClymonts and their mum, which means I get the better car and a tour guide who is on his best behaviour. Our tour guide is a cocky soldier called Bevan from Queensland. Apparently, driving cars is not his specialty, but he was so keen to get to Iraq that he sent in an 'expression of interest' to come over no matter what was on offer. He is full of cheeky charm and dry observations. As we drive past Saddam's son

Uday's palace, Bevan takes enormous pleasure in showing us the great hole in the roof that killed him.

'The Americans sent him an eviction notice in the form of a JDAM missile,' Bevan explains.

'Did Uday get his bond back?' I ask flatly. Bevan doesn't laugh. Some people enjoy being the only funny one.

Toni McClymont has to be dropped at Australian HQ. As she jumps out of the four-wheel drive Bevan remarks, 'Toni, are you sure you want to leave me alone with your daughters?'

Quick as a flash she says, 'It's okay. I know their type.' Laughter all round, but not from Bevan.

The Australian HQ in Baghdad is inside one of Saddam's hunting palaces. The interior is ornate marble contradicted by army-issue water containers and bunk beds jammed into hallways that were once traversed by visiting heads of state. Surfing the internet involves sitting on a plush yet gaudy-looking gold chair with a red velvet seat and back. *Fit for a King, literally.* When you look through the finely decorated windows all you can see are sandbags. Underneath a giant chandelier in another room is a flat screen with MTV playing to a few tired-looking soldiers lazing around on a break.

Is this what it's like to be in a war? You can't hear any gunfire or explosions, yet here I am in Baghdad. When one of the guys from the RAAF band gets back from lunch he says he heard a round whiz past when he was walking from the DFAC. No one believes him, but he's sticking to his story.

———

That night we perform on an outdoor stage. There aren't many Australians on this base so they invite their American friends as well. The soldiers are already sitting on benches out in the cold half an hour before the show even starts. *Gee, they're keen!* All the performers are starting to reflect their tour experiences in the show. Adrian wears a helmet on stage and does an impression of a tank with his didgeridoo. *Howls of laughter.* Then I come out.

'Are there any Americans in?' *Big cheer.* 'To you, I just want to say thank you for supporting Australia's war in Iraq!' *Silence, followed by hysterical laughter from the Australians.* The Americans completely outnumber the Australians in the audience, which makes this funnier. Then I start to make fun of the ISOPREP form used to identify you when you've been taken hostage. I realised everyone in the audience would have filled one out too.

'What's your favourite colour? *Green*. What's the name of your first dog? *Fluffy*. How am I going to remember this shit when people around me are being shot with a shotgun?' I yell. 'That's a bit too much pressure for me!' *The crowd convulses with laughter.* I am loving it. Thank you, good night from me, and then the McClymonts bring it home.

Lieutenant Colonel Greg pulls me aside after the show and says, 'How did you feel about that?'

When this is posed to a comedian it is always a loaded question. 'Great!' I reply.

'You know how I said you have to be careful about OPSEC?' *That's operational security.* 'That thing about the ISOPREP form, you're going to have to drop that. You see these speakers your microphone is connected to? They can be heard outside the camp.' *Right.* 'It was pretty funny though,' Greg says with a smile that tells me he is not a kill-joy. It's just his job.

I don't waste much time ringing home and telling Ellie that I have to drop a bit of my routine because it is a threat to national security. Not many comedians can say that.

Earlier that afternoon when I was inspecting the stage set-up I met a young GI named Nat. He whizzed up to me on a mountain bike and asked me what was going on. 'There's a show on tonight,' I tell him.

'I'll bring my buddies,' he says.

Nat looks like a kid in a stack hat who has ridden his mountain bike straight out of the suburbs of America, except that he's wearing cammo and has an M16 strapped across his back. He looks all of 20, except for his eyeballs which look like they have been plucked out of a 50-year-old man's head and inserted into his young boy's face. He has a vacant stare; the relaxed irises of a boy who has already seen too much. His face is relatively expressionless, even though his voice is quite animated. It gives him a quality that would make him seem Australian if it weren't for his accent.

When we finish the show, Nat comes back with his buddies. They loved it. 'Can we meet the girls?' he asks. This is a role I never became comfortable with – being a McClymont chaperone. 'If they want, me and my buddies can go back and get our Humvee to show them!'

Nat is quite excited, not like a man who hasn't seen a civilian woman for months, more like a primary school kid who wants to impress a girl in his class by showing her his Tonka toy.

'Why not?' I say. We continue packing up and soon Nat and his mates are back with their heavily fortified Humvee patrol vehicle. It's one thing to see military hardware at an army open day, but it's another to see one that has been busy in a war that same day. Nat's buddies have the same vacant stare, but they seem to be entranced by the soft lightness and beauty of the McClymonts, who proceed to climb into the vehicle of war to get photos. Nat shows us his body armour that weighs twice as much as ours. They have to wear it inside this truck when they patrol around Baghdad. The Humvee has a big square piece of black metal, the size of a large floor tile, which is attached to the end of a long boom at the front of the truck. It is folded up like a retracted boom gate at a toll booth. I ask Nat what it's for.

'This plate has the same heat index as the engine. So if we drive over a thermally detonating explosive device the bomb goes off a couple of seconds earlier, which means that it blows the front of the truck off instead of us,' he explains blankly.

Can you imagine folding down that boom each day before you go out on patrol, knowing why it's there? A seatbelt is one thing but a thermal plate that makes an explosion less likely to be fatal? The distant stares are starting to make sense. Nat and his buddies would have chatted to us all night if they could. I think we made them forget for a small moment that they were there.

Warrant Officer Andrew gathers us up and tells Nat that we have to get going. 'Are you sure you can't stay a little longer? We could show you around tomorrow,' they plead. But we have to go. On the way back to our hunting palace Andrew tells us that a lot of the ADF are university educated, but the American Army are mostly uneducated and from the poorer areas in the south. Nat and his buddies have stepped way outside of their comfort zone and are over here for a tour of duty that lasts for a year. Little did they know that this tour was about to get extended by George Bush.

When I get back to my accommodation I ring Ellie. The phone call is free. You just pick up the phone and dial the number like you were in Australia, no country code or anything. It's a weird chat. My girlfriend is talking on the phone with all the weighty tones of someone who has received a phone call from a war zone. I try to reassure her by talking about the lattes, doughnuts and Baskin-Robbins ice-cream, but leave out the bits about flak jackets, shrapnel-proof sunglasses and my location. Have you ever tried talking to someone on the phone while not telling them where you are? It's pretty tricky.

'We had a good show here at *this* base. I can't wait til we fly out tomorrow to *another* base,' I tell her. 'Oh, I'll explain it when I get back.' It's hard to reassure your loved ones that you're okay when you can't disclose your location for OPSEC reasons. The imagination takes over. I start thinking that maybe I can extend my trip and spend another couple of months in Thailand. I'd be lying on the beach, while lying on the phone, 'Hello, Ellie? This tour is taking ages. I can't tell you my exact location for my own safety.'

That night, back at Australian HQ, I climb into my bunk exhausted. Those bunk beds I saw jammed in the hallway are ours! The women sleep separately. I'm with Lieutenant Colonel Greg, Warrant Officer Andrew, Adrian, Alan and the boys in the RAAF band. We have the magical combination of a late night and an early wake-up. *Great.* Just as I'm about to fall asleep I discover we have a snorer in our midst. This can cause problems, but I am too tired to be annoyed. Off I go. *Lights are out.*

I wake up with a start. Where am I? *Oh, Baghdad. No worries.* It's surprising how quickly it all becomes so normal. We go and have a giant breakfast in the giant dining facility, then it's off to the International Zone, or IZ, in another part of Baghdad. There are a few Australians there who need cheering up apparently. The McClymonts, a few of the band members and I will fly over to the IZ by helicopter, while Adrian, Alan and the rest stay back for a barbecue and a small show here at Australian HQ. I'm told the helicopter ride will be a big thrill. One soldier tells me not to muck around and go ahead and put Wagner on the iPod and live out my *Apocalypse Now* fantasies.

It's a beautiful, sunny winter's day at the helipad. We see some US gunships come in to land. Soldiers get on and the aircrafts take off. It's very noisy and very spectacular. This is going to be a lot of fun, but fun in a still-needing-to-wear-a-flak-jacket-just-in-case kind of way. A bit like bungee-jumping, but with a sniper taking pot shots at you. A couple more gunships come in and land, soldiers get on and then they take off again. *We're on the next one, apparently.* Helicopters land and take off again. *The next one, apparently.* Helicopters land and take off. *It's okay, we're on the next one.*

L to R Me, Alan Caswell, Warrant Officer Andrew Kelly, Brooke McClymont, Sam McClymont, Molly McClymont and Toni McClymont, Adrian Ross and Lieutenant Colonel Greg McCauley

One of Saddam's hunting palaces seen from Australian HQ

Hurry up and wait

A couple of stickers for sale. The Hard Rock Café Baghdad one is a joke (I think ...)

The pirates of Baghdad

Traffic laws still apply in a war zone

Australian HQ balcony

Three American Humvees parallel-parked at the Ziggurat

In a war zone people need souvenirs

Brooke in the turret of an ASLAV

My ASLAV's skid marks

Live on stage in Tarin Kowt, Afghanistan

Stand up on 'the boat'

GIs on top of the Ziggurat

Machine gun on the Ziggurat

We've been sitting in the dirt on the side of the helipad for about five hours when it's decided that we can't get to the IZ, as the helicopters are too busy. I don't know what 'busy' means but I'm happy not to be involved. This is where I learn the meaning of 'hurry up and wait', a common phrase in army lingo. It seems that's what you do: turn up half an hour early for things that run late by hours. It doesn't bother me really. I never understand people who get annoyed by waiting. When you're waiting all you have to do is sit around and do nothing. That's exactly what you do on holiday. The way I see it, waiting is just a tiny unscheduled holiday.

As they still wanted a show at the IZ, and as we couldn't get there by helicopter, we're told that the RAAF band will go instead by convoy along Route Irish. We were informed about Route Irish on our first day. It's the most direct route between the Australian HQ and the IZ; it's also the most dangerous road in Baghdad. The misty mornings are the worst, because the mist allows the insurgents to sneak out and lay improvised explosive devices, or IEDs, on the road. We find out that the band will go instead of us because the ADF are not prepared to risk endangering the 'talent' on any open roads outside the camps. I really feel sorry for the band because they're under orders. Suddenly, joining the military because it was the only way to still play music, live in subsidised housing and have a dental plan didn't seem like such a grand choice. Luckily, the RAAF band does a bit of 'hurrying up and waiting' themselves and ends up not going to the IZ after all. They get the night off and the IZ misses out on a show.

In the end, we put on a little show and a barbecue to about 50 Australians back on the balcony of Australian HQ. It's fun because there are no Americans in the audience so I can dig in. I do a bit of material about how some of the GIs are so fat that they don't need flak jackets; if they get shot the bullet will be lucky to touch the rib cage. *Much laughter.* Then I announce that tonight I am going to have a Hurry Up and Wait Party at 11 pm. 'Everyone turns up half an hour early. You wait around for a few hours and THEN THE FUN NEVER STARTS!' It is a great night.

While on stage the small lake beside Australian HQ attracts my attention. In the middle of the lake is a small island with a golf green and a flag. What is it? Next day I find out.

We get up early so that we can be ready to 'hurry up and wait', I presume. After breakfast I meet a friendly young Australian soldier named Damian. He has black woolly hair and a roguish smile. He gives me an auto-graphed photo of himself, which makes him appeal straightaway.

'Do you want to become a pirate of Baghdad?' he asks.

This weirdo is right on my wavelength. 'Of course!' I yell.

Damian and his mates take me downstairs and hand me a golf club. He tees up a ball and points to a little island through the morning mist. 'Aim for the flag,' he says. I have a whack and the ball falls short in the water.

'Have another go,' Damian offers. I have another whack and I'm on the green. 'All right. Grab your putter but before you do, put on this bandanna and eye patch.'

How can I resist this strange little man? Okay. This is where it gets ridiculous. Damian invites Brooke, Sam, Molly, Adrian and me into a small dinghy. Now here was a bit of Aussie ingenuity, because in place of an outboard the dinghy has a whipper snipper with a homemade propeller attached to the end of it. To say it was slow is an understatement. It would have been faster if we'd used an eggbeater. In fact, it would have been faster if we'd used teaspoons for oars. Actually, it would have been faster if we'd used oars. When we finally arrive on the island I get the ball in on five. *My short game has always been my failing.* When the ball goes in the hole, Damian yells, 'I now pronounce you a Pirate of Baghdad!' We take a photo that I'm promised will go on the pirate board, and then we whipper-snipper our way back to shore. *Too funny.*

There's no time to enjoy our new pirate status. We head straight off for some sightseeing. We're taken to see some more of Saddam's palaces. It's quite a long drive but we are still within the Green Zone. We stop to take a look at the twin palaces: one called Victory Over Iran and the other, which is incomplete, called Victory Over America. Iraq lost the Iran–Iraq war in the '80s and they came off second best in Gulf War I. Of course, the Australian army tour guide takes great satisfaction in pointing this out to us. What he doesn't mention is that America still seems to celebrate the 'stalemate' in Vietnam and that we have a national holiday for a failed beach landing in Gallipoli.

You see, on my trip I seem to encounter two different types of military personnel. There are the ones like our tour guide who take gratification in telling us that even though the palaces look extravagant, if you peel off the outer marble all this shoddy workmanship is revealed underneath. This heavy-handed metaphor is used to emphasise that Saddam was all about outward appearances and that he had it coming to him. Then there's the other military types who will pick a quiet moment to say *thanks for coming over* and that *just because you're in a war doesn't mean you support it*. I met more soldiers that fell into this camp than the former. This either means that the majority of soldiers didn't want to be there or, more likely, that people like to tell you what you want to hear. Cynics of a feather flock together.

When I walk amongst the palace rubble I feel like I am in history. I put a piece of marble in my pocket as a souvenir to give to Ellie when I return home. Not many people can say they've got a piece of marble from one of Saddam's palaces. The walls in this opulent palace are defaced. 'I love Stacey' is spray-painted incongruously on the wall. There is Arabic graffiti too, though none of us can read it. It could have said anything from DEATH TO AMERICA to I LOVE BASKIN-ROBBINS for all we knew.

But it is when we climbed up to the top of the palace roof that I see one of the most beautiful sights since arriving here. I see green. Not khaki green. Green grass. Not just any green grass. It is green grass that's all over the outer perimeter. I am looking at Iraq – a green field

in Iraq. There is no one in it but it is Iraq nonetheless.
It turns out to be the only actual part of Iraq I would
see for my entire trip.

7

TALLIL
SATURDAY, 23 DECEMBER 2006

We head back to Baghdad Airport to fly to another base in Southern Iraq. We are in a mad rush to get to the airport. Could this be the 'hurry up' that precedes the 'wait'? It turns out my suspicions were well founded. We get to the airport around midday and sit down on some concrete in the middle of the airfield and wait for the plane. We end up waiting on the tarmac for six hours. But you know what? It was a fun six hours.

Tell me, when do you ever find yourself hanging out with such entertaining people, with no alcohol, no mobile phones and nothing to amuse you except each other – and all the time in the world. It was like being a kid again. The McClymonts and I play cards, Celebrity Heads (we don't have any pens or cardboard so we whisper the celebrity to each other), and hopscotch. We even build a catapult to see how high we can launch objects in the hangar. I manage to fling a water bottle about six metres up in the air!

After a very busy day wasting time we're finally told that the Hercules can't make it today and that we'll have to fly out tomorrow. We get into the minibus and start heading back to the Australian HQ in what is becoming heavy rain. The minibus is sliding all over the road when there's a call on the only mobile, belonging to Lieutenant Colonel Greg.

'We're back on!' he yells and off to the airport we go again. They are desperate to get us out that night. We board the Hercules and it takes off abruptly. I dig into my *Flags of Our Fathers* book to really get the war mood happening.

On this leg of the flight I am sitting next to Molly. When we're up in the air there is a flash of white light out the side of the plane, at which point Molly jumps into my lap. We are reassured that it's no big deal. Apparently they just shoot flares out the side of the

Hercules on the off chance that someone has shot an RPG at them. *Thank god for that!* My ring unclenches slightly.

I ask Lieutenant Colonel Greg, 'If there had been an actual RPG you would tell us, right?'

He looks at me, then over to little Molly, then looks back at me again and says, 'Yes.' *Not very convincing.* I know what is happening straightaway. On this trip I am going to have to survive on the amount of information that would not alarm a 19-year-old girl from Grafton.

We are flying to Tallil in Southern Iraq to entertain the Overwatch Battle Group (West). This is Australia's infantry, all 550 of them. (Postscript: They are no longer there. They've left like the Japanese engineers who were in the camp before them. They were stationed there for security and to train the Iraqi Army.) In Baghdad we were told that these soldiers are the real deal. They get shot at and they shoot people. *Good.* I am sick of entertaining softy diplomats and cushy admin people in the Green Zone.

It is almost midnight by the time we land. The headlights of the minibus aren't giving much away except that we're in a mud bowl. The desert sand is very fine, like dust. It's either 45 degrees Celsius and the sand gets in your ears and your nose, or it's like it is now – cold, and when the rain hits the dust it turns into a sticky clay. It's shit either way. After sliding sideways for most of the way the minibus pulls into the headquarters of the Australian section.

We drag our tired arses past the big concrete walls that are for blast protection and into the Australian HQ, a small temporary hut built of plywood. We fall in for 'a brief'. Now this is the army's cruel joke, because although they are called 'a brief' they never are. The army has to explain everything in the most miniscule detail, so even the least bright man in the infantry can follow what's going on. Captain Nathan is in charge of this infantry and fortunately takes one look at our half-cut eyes and says that he will spare us the details because we look like we are ready for some much-needed sleep. And frankly our attention span at this time of night is pretty much zero.

So off we trudge to find our tents. That's right – tents! We are roughing it in tents. But I have to admit they do have central heating and beds. We hit the hay in our relatively frontier accommodation and are out like a light.

When I wake up the next morning the tent is empty. Everyone has gone. They must have let me sleep in. No complaints there. Then I realise that I might miss breakfast. *Shit!* It will be a long wait to lunch. I walk outside and it's a gloomy overcast day. I take a look around the camp and there's mud everywhere. Duckboards have been placed over the mud to create walkways. It reminds me of the Somme, but in this mud your main fear is losing a shoe, not your life.

'Where's the DFAC?' I ask the first soldier I see.

'About half a kilometre that way. You sure you don't want to wait for the bus?' he offers.

'Nah, I'll walk.' Off I go.

I walk for a bit until I come to a sentry at a boom gate. The first thing I think is: Does this mean that breakfast is outside the wire? 'No,' the sentry reassures me. The further I walk the more mud I pick up on my boots, and I am beginning to build up a comical-looking large pair of mud clogs. I start to see endless puddles of water between me and my destination. *Maybe I should've waited for the bus.* I keep tiptoeing on tiny land bridges between the puddles until I finally get to the DFAC. I feel like I've just navigated through a minefield where the worst-case scenario was a wet sock. I sign into the DFAC as Dennis Lillee and sit down to breakfast on my own.

The dining area is in the last stages of breakfast except for a couple of stragglers. One thing I've enjoyed about my trip to all these bases is that it is impossible to dine alone. You can sit by yourself in the most isolated part of the dining facility and people will always sit next to you to try to find out what's been going on. On this morning, an Australian platoon up stumps and plonk themselves around me. 'Can't let you eat on your own, mate!' comes the introduction.

After a bit of chitchat about the show and my trip so far, we finish up and the oldest-looking guy in the group chimes in, 'Do you want a lift back?' *Of course I do.*

We go out the front of the DFAC and I discover that they drive around in a light-armoured vehicle known as an ASLAV (Australian Light Armoured Vehicle). It's like a tank with tyres. You see them in the news, usually after one of them has driven over a roadside bomb. 'Jump in the turret and put on a helmet!' the one in charge offers.

It was one of those moments that summarised this trip for me. I'm in a tank in Iraq and I haven't even gotten the sleep out of my eyes yet. This vehicle's crew know that I'm half asleep and bewildered because through the cans they keep making comments like, 'This'll wake him up!' and 'You're not in Melbourne now, are ya?!' They drive me back to HQ where I find the rest of my group surrounded by about five ASLAVs. Molly, Sam and Brooke are all putting on helmets, with several men queuing up to provide assistance. Alan and Adrian have to work out how to strap on their helmet themselves. Looks like we're about to go off on some adventure!

Before we drive off, the battle group commander thanks us. I'll never forget what he said. 'Thanks for giving up your Christmas to come over here and spend it with us. Now, I know that there has been a lot of fuss made back home as to whether it is right or wrong for entertainers to come over here and support the troops. We appreciate that you have made a soldier's choice. A soldier goes to battle not because he agrees with why he's going but because he is there to do his job.' *Well said.* This was more than just the old 'support our diggers' argument. The commander had a knowing look that told me: *none* of us think we should be here.

We travel in convoy. Alan and I are in one ASLAV, Brooke and Sam in another, and Molly and Adrian in another. For such bulky armour-plated vehicles they've got some speed in them. Matthew is in charge of the vehicle I'm in and tells me he's going to take us down to the range to fire off a few rounds. *Yay! I suppose.* As I find out, this is all the shooting they get to do. Matthew tells me what a frustrating job the soldiers have in Southern Iraq, because they've got all the hardware and training but they aren't allowed to go out and do anything in case any Australians die and make John Howard look bad. How quickly things can change. (Of course all these soldiers survived their tour of duty, but John Howard didn't survive the election.)

We queue up at the range like cars waiting to get into a car wash. The range is pretty much a giant pile of dirt that you fire your machine-gun into. Finally, it's our turn. Now, I'm a farm boy. I've fired a .22 and a .222. A .222 rifle has a bit of kick and it can give you a start, but this thing was on a whole other level. First of all, you can paint your target. This means you can position a digital point with a laser on a moving target, so that when you and your target are moving you can put a steady stream of fire onto it. Suddenly, the ANZAC trick of putting a periscope on the side of a .303 doesn't look so special. The bullets and their cartridges are the size of the fattest texta you can get at a newsagent. And when I fire the gun it is so loud that part of me wants to cry. *My Xbox is looking lame now.* Tracer fire is spitting out and some of it sizzles for a few seconds after it hits the dirt and the magnesium inside burns out. As I'm firing, cartridges and clips are pouring all over the roof of the ASLAV like water. I'm wasting a lot of the government's money. I'm whizzing through tax returns. I think I shoot my whole HECS debt into that pile of mud!

I've fired a machine gun in Iraq. Not many civilians get to throw that around in a conversation. *What next?*

'Do you want to have a drive?' Matthew asks me.

'Are you sure?'

He doesn't miss a beat. 'Don't worry. It's automatic!' And it was! If you've ever wondered how to drive a tank, I'll tell you. You take off the handbrake, put the tank from 'Park' into 'Drive', take your foot off the brake and push down the accelerator, and off you go. For a machine that weighs a few tons it moves quick. I have my head poking out the hatch and I am driving a tank in Iraq. *I AM DRIVING A TANK IN IRAQ!*

I'm thinking that I really have to learn how to say no. A series of tiny sensible decisions has added up to a ludicrous situation. I drag race against another tank that is driven by one of the women in their unit, and she beats me just to prove that equal opportunity is alive and well in the Australian Army.

Matthew asks me, 'Do you want to go over there?'

I'm like, 'But there are no roads over there.' *Exactly. Off I went.*

'Make sure you hook in!' he yells. With that I put my foot to the floor. What a thrill! I'm not shy. My inner farm boy is in full flight as I do a doughnut. *I DID A DOUGHNUT IN A TANK IN IRAQ!* It is definitely a day of firsts.

<hr/>

When I get back from a day of cheap – well, more like expensive – thrills, it is time for a shower. This turns into one of the more pointless exercises of my trip. The shower block is 500 metres away, on duckboards, over mud. When you're in the shower, it is just a beautiful brief moment in time where you can warm up your bones and pretend you are elsewhere. Then you change into a fresh pair of clothes for the muddy walk back to your tent. In the end, you're slightly cosier inside your fresh undies, but your exterior looks much the same as before you had your shower.

We are all looking forward to the show tonight. It will be in a big recreational tent with about 300 Australian infantry and a few American guests. The infantry has a reputation for being boisterous so I'm looking forward to this gig. Everyone is in good spirits because it's Christmas Eve. *Did I not mention that?* Days really lose their significance over here.

That night on stage, I start off with a bit of, 'I didn't know there would be so many women over here?' *The women give a bit of a cheer.* 'I heard that you're all lesbians.' *This gets a big cheer from the majority male crowd.* Not my proudest moment. Then I cap it off with a very old joke that I wouldn't bother with back home. 'I don't have a problem with lesbians. I love your work. I've got all your magazines and DVDs.' *The place goes off.* Not my cleverest moment, but I had a feeling there were no critics from *The Age* in tonight.

Then I do a bit of 'local', as comedians call it. 'I love it here. You see, back at home my bathroom is right near my bedroom, which is STUPID. I'm going to change that. I'm going to build myself a new bathroom 500 metres away through mud. That'll be heaps better!'

After the show I'm not feeling too crash hot. I'm starting to get a cold. I suppose jumping from the Australian summer into the Middle Eastern winter isn't good for you. I tell Lieutenant Colonel Greg because I'm mainly worried about others in the group getting sick and having a miserable time. He refers me to the camp doctor, who is helpful. He says to me in his surgery, 'Whatever you want, we've got it.'

I walk in to the medical department and it is like a giant Priceline Pharmacy minus the price. They tell me that they're more than happy to help because, as no one is getting shot, they are left with nothing to do. So I ask for some strong painkillers and a couple of Strepsils and then go to bed early. I want to get better quickly also, as we all know, the earlier you go to bed, the sooner Christmas arrives.

When I wake up the next morning I find a present at the end of my bed. We have a kris kringle among the performers. I had brought some big bags of lollies from Australia that I gave as a present because I thought they would be hard to find over here. *How wrong was I?* My present is a gorilla in army uniform from a souvenir shop and the McClymonts give the guys in the RAAF band their self-titled CD as a present. Luckily the band likes their music.

I pop a lozenge in my mouth, then go outside to celebrate Christmas in the mud. The sun has come out, which is a luxury and the troops have gathered around the centre of the camp near the office HQ to do a kris kringle of their own. Everyone is there and everyone is into it. After a lot of gifts that had been bought within the camp were handed out, there were a few gifts that had been purchased on holidays.

You see, in the middle of a six-month tour in the army you get a two-week break. Where you go is up to you. Some go home to their families, while others go away for a fortnight of partying in Europe. So out comes a present of a blow-up doll. Much laughter. Then comes a gift of a male blow-up doll. More laughter. Some of the women at the camp are given a vibrator. Everyone is equal in the army. Then there's a pressie that makes me laugh a bit too much. If you've seen the Graham Kennedy film about Vietnam called the *Odd Angry Shot* you'll know what I mean. The Padre of the camp is given a wanking machine. It is a shoebox with a hole in the end. When you open it up you can see a peacock feather inside that can be rotated by a handle at the other end. From the volume of laughter I'm guessing that the film is a favourite.

While everyone is basking in the afterglow of a kris

kringle well-kringled, I think I will sneak in a phone call back home before the queue gets too long. The last thing I want to do is tie up the phone line when people who have been away for a genuinely long time need to check in with their loved ones.

When I get to the phones though, no one is there. I have them all to myself! After a call to Ellie, I ring my dad. My family is having their Christmas lunch. Dad tells me to stay safe and then passes me onto Mum, who handballs me straight onto my sister Cathy. I think they imagine I am paying for the phone call, but even after I try to explain to my other sister Mary that there is no rush, I am flung onto my brother Phil, then my other brother Nick, and then onto my brother-in-law Rob. Then it is all over. I think I wish my entire family a Merry Christmas in less than a minute. I would be happy to chat for longer, but my family seem to be treating the call like it is an emergency. Either that or I'm the least favourite family member and finding out that I was going to a war zone over Christmas was the best present they could ever receive.

What do you do on Christmas when your family is not about? Whatever you damn well please. The camp is holding a poker tournament for this very reason. Ten dollars in. Winner takes all. There are about 60 starters. One of the benefits of being in the middle of nowhere with a lot of idle minds is that if something is on – IT IS ON. That's why the shows are so great. If a show's on everyone turns up. There is no, 'Sorry I'm doing something else, too busy.' Everyone is just there. And people don't do things by halves. That is my only explanation for seeing some of the poker players in full lounge suits with casual slip-ons tiptoeing through the mud to the poker tent. They look like a yobbo version of *Ocean's Eleven* making their way through the mud.

There are about eight tables, which an hour or so later are whittled down to four, and then on and on it goes. There are some good players and others who are just in it to win it. Either way, a couple more hours later and I get down to the last table. Now this is no casino, so we don't have any higher-value chips. As a result, we all have mountains of chips to negotiate. Racks and racks of one-dollar chips kept getting put to the side from earlier rounds. The blinds keep getting raised and I am forced to go all in, and get knocked out. So it comes down to two. One is an older-looking man who has a shaved head like Robert Duvall in *Apocalypse Now*. The other man is the only Asian man I've seen in the Australian military for my entire trip. You'll never guess what happens – the Asian guy wins. In this tournament I had put bets on myself, but maybe I should have betted on the stereotype.

The 40 or so men who are in charge of training the Iraqi Army invite Brooke and me to have Christmas lunch with them. As they put it, they are the 'lovers' while the infantry are the 'fighters'. When we arrive at their common room it is obvious that they have gone to a lot of trouble. There are Christmas decorations up, table settings for everyone, there's even a barbecued chook in place of a turkey and those hotdogs again to replace sausages. In these conditions it is all quite a treat. We even get bonbons with crap jokes inside to really make us feel at home. I make a few crap jokes of my own, mainly at the expense of one of the guys who keeps goading me with his constant requests of 'tell us a joke!'

Rugby is the football of choice for the army. Back in Australia, there's a big base in Townsville and a lot of soldiers go through Duntroon in Canberra. This means that the majority of the army comes from New South Wales and Queensland. Aussie Rules may have been played at the base of the Pyramids in World War I, but things have changed. There is a big Christmas Day touch footy clash to be played out in the drying mud between the officers and the grunts. Apparently it is a game to settle some old scores.

I'm invited to help out with the commentary. Dougie, clearly the camp joker and very popular with the crowd, is doing the main commentary and I'm on special comments, which prove tricky. Have you ever tried to commentate a game where you don't know any of the players' names? Dougie is on fire. He makes a comment over the PA that the camp commander, Captain Nathan, has been waxing his legs in preparation for the game (he is not very hairy).

Upon finding out it is a young lad's birthday I call out, 'Happy Birthday! You were born on Christmas Day, who do you think you are? Jesus? His mother was a virgin. Yours wasn't, Dougie will tell you that!' *It gets a laugh. That's good enough for me. Sometimes you do what you have to do to get over the line.*

While I'm sitting in the commentary booth, which is really just a bench, sharing a mic with Dougie, I can see these boys running around having a great time. That's what they are, boys. Some of them were born in 1987. And while I'm up in the booth sharing jokes with Dougie I can't help but think that nothing has changed.

We agree to invade countries without UN approval, and then we send in our expendable youth to do the jobs of our so-called men in Canberra.

We do another show that night. It's fun performing to an audience that you feel you've gotten to know. We tell stories about how we allegedly drove and fired a tank. (We don't want anyone to get into trouble.) And the audience is already quite spirited because they've all been given two cans of beer for Christmas. The cans are tall and go a long way when you haven't had a drink in a couple of months. The cruel part is that the British supplied them, so they gave them Fosters thinking that's what Australians would want – of course we all know how that ends. I give them a pretty loose show as the two Fosters and painkillers are doing amazing things for my performance.

On our last morning in Tallil we are offered the chance to do a little bit of sightseeing. The Padre asks us if we want to go to the Ziggurat, the birthplace of Abraham. It's a man-made monument, older than the Pyramids. Yeah sure, I'm in. On the way, I meet the only Iraqis that I will meet for the whole trip. By 'meet' I mean our conversation goes like this:

'Do you want to buy DVD?' they say.

'No,' I say.

We drop in at the International Market. This market was set up so that local merchants could sell things to the soldiers. This works well as Iraq's currency is now US dollars. If I told you that I went to a market in the Middle East you'd imagine something exotic, which is not where I was. The market is a compound surrounded by earthen walls to absorb any explosions. Inside there are about half a dozen stalls run by locals who have been checked and rechecked. On sale are carpets and rugs, and you can organise your purchase to be shipped back to Australia. Cigars are also a favourite and just the ticket if you want to go for that despot look. The thing that catches my eye though is all the DVDs. I can buy the entire *Sopranos* television series for five dollars. You can buy a DVD of a film that has just been released in America the previous day. You gotta love the inter-net. It invaded Iraq long before we did. In the fog of war, video piracy doesn't seem very serious.

The Ziggurat is amazing. In peacetime, apparently, it was one of the largest tourist attractions in Iraq. The birthplace of Abraham is significant for a lot of religions and the upside of the war is that we have it to ourselves.

It is really impressive. To my untrained eye it kind of looks like the Mayan pyramids in Central America or what I imagine they might look like. Straightaway our group succumbs to our Western desires and we start to climb the thing. When we get to the top the view is marvellous. We can see our camp, even though we are still inside it (I think we are in some kind of exclusion zone); we can also see the ripple of the creased earth in all directions. And right on top of this ancient piece of earthworks we find three GIs with a ripped fold-up Bunnings chair, which they take in turns to sit on. Is there anywhere on Earth that this giant hardware chain hasn't penetrated?

The three soldiers are fully armed which always has the effect of reminding me that I could get shot. They are providing security for a group of Christian soldiers holding a service down below. There are soldiers who believe they are over here to fight a crusade. Some of those absurd sound bites that you palm off as being 'George Bush going at it again' can represent millions of Americans' opinion. There are Christian soldiers from the south who believe they are fighting the good fight. If enough people believe it, it's true, I suppose. At one of the camps there is a model of the twin towers with the inscription: 'Remember Why We're Here'. That's right, according to some we invaded Iraq because Al Qaeda ran some planes into a building. *What are they thinking? Near enough's good enough? Let's kill tens of thousands of the wrong people to avenge the deaths of less than three thousand?* If enough people believe it, it's true. Here I am standing at the birthplace of Abraham in the middle of a modern crusade. I am getting so much more out of this trip than just a few happy snaps.

8

SECRET COUNTRY NO. 2
TUESDAY, 26 DECEMBER 2006

When we say goodbye to the men at Tallil it is sad.
When you spend Christmas with someone it creates a
bond.

Next, we fly to another country that I can't mention.
There they have a huge US airbase. The country that
I can't mention doesn't mind having a US presence
there, but it would not be good PR if other countries
knew about it. I suppose it's a little bit like having the
unpopular guy from the office at your party, but you
don't want to advertise the fact that he is there.

While I am in this country, officially I am 'nowhere'.

Have you ever been nowhere before? It's a funny feeling. For me, my time here is spent constantly walking around in a spooky fashion going, 'I'm nowhere ... wooooo! I'm noooooo ... wheeeeeere ... wooooo!' I keep doing it until I even start to annoy myself.

Once we land in 'nowhere' we are allowed to hand in our flak jackets because they aren't needed here. It turns out that America isn't at war with 'nowhere', so it is a lot safer place to be. I'd hate 'nowhere' to get complacent though, because after you've declared a war on drugs and a war on terrorism, 'nowhere' should be shaking in its boots. When we walk across the tarmac we are greeted with the gentle sounds of Lee Kernaghan cascading through the speakers across the bitumen. The McClymonts are going to go down a treat at this gig.

'Nowhere' is a huge US Airbase and Recreational Camp and it's also where the RAAF is based in the area of operations. Now, when I say the RAAF is based here it makes it sound grand. However, I can't stress how *small* our detachment is. We can fit our entire air force presence into one of the US Air Force's smaller planes. Australia's two Hercules planes are maintained here in 'nowhere'. We have been flown in to entertain the ground crew of about 60 Australians.

When we drive through the camp it is luxurious. Essentially, it is a holiday camp for US troops who take their two-week break from combat. They all walk around in standard-issue tracksuits with a reflective strip to prevent them from getting run over. *Safety first!* There's nothing worse than being hit by a motor vehicle when you're trained to be shot. The camp itself is impeccable. Rows upon rows as far as the eye can see of perfectly aligned, temporary buildings all connected by perfectly edged white gravel paths. It sounds like it has all the charm of an asylum, but after being in the mud at Tallil this is Nirvana. Here you can have a shower and *stay clean* — maybe even do some laundry! *Oh, the simple pleasures.* We retire to our accommodation, which are big semi-permanent tents with central heating, and get ready for the show.

The gig tonight is a funny one. It's only for a few Australians and will be held outdoors in the little Australian area where everyone is having a barbecue. The RAAF band is pared back to the bare bones, so it kind of has this vibe of a university cafeteria gig.

Lieutenant Colonel Greg pulls me aside before I go on and says, 'You know that material you had about the ISOPREP hostage forms? Well, you can do that joke here. In fact, do it here because it was very funny.' He has a point. If a tree falls in the forest, does it make a sound? And so it follows that if a comedian does a banned joke in a country he's not in, does the joke exist? Surely I can't breach security in a country I'm not in?

It is a fun gig either way, but it gets even better afterwards because they have a bar and the bar has beer. The air force informs us that they are a bit more sophisticated than the army, who can't be trusted with beer. That said, there is a strict three-beer limit per person, which is accounted for on a card system.

That night the gig had gone so well that no one seemed to care about the three-beer limit cards, so it was Crown Lagers all round. Alan is beside himself. His usual flushed red face had started to calm down from his enforced abstinence so he is desperate to get his cheeks pink again. Adrian hangs around to keep an eye on Alan. Brooke even has a beer or two and Sam and Molly each have one in a show of support.

Toni McClymont leaves me in charge of her daughters because they need to be looked after in this all-male environment. You don't have to be a paranoid mother to see this. I promptly let her down. We all intended to go back together, but four beers does amazing things after time off the job. Adrian and I were flat out trying to get Alan to stop drinking and walk away from the alcohol. The McClymonts and I get split up and I just have to presume that they'll get home. The last I saw they were chatting to some reasonably polite air force guys. *Surely I could trust them? I won't be seeing the young Grafton girls to their door but they're adults, right?*

Later that night I realise that Alan must have got back all right because I can hear him snoring. *The phantom snorer was him all along!* But I find it hard to get to sleep as I worry about the McClymonts in worst-case scenarios and how I failed in my duty of care.

In the morning I see the girls at breakfast and they seem fine. 'What did you get up to last night?' I ask.

'We just chatted to those cute boys and they were nice enough to give us a lift back to our accommodation,' Brooke says matter-of-factly.

I apologise profusely to Toni, but in her no-nonsense way she says, 'That's okay, but just don't forget that you let me down.'

I really like Toni, so I feel terrible.

After our night of celebration, we're set for a tour today of the airfield. It is HUGE. I mean, I can't stress enough how huge it is. If everything is bigger in America, then everything in the American military is bigger again. We see some amazing things like fighter jets whizzing around like in *Top Gun*, moments that would have made for great photos, but of course for security reasons no photographs are allowed. We see some C17s that are the standard transport jet in the US Air Force. They do the equivalent job of our Hercules but are massive and jet-powered and make our propeller-powered Hercules look like a Cessna. The C17s were used during the original invasion of Iraq to parachute-in Humvees like they were food-aid packages, though they obviously had the opposite effect. The interior of this jet is so large that it can carry four helicopters, if you fold them up the right way.

We see fighter jets taking off at really steep angles. If they took off any steeper they would look like a space shuttle going straight up. And yes, the reason behind this angle of take-off is to minimise the risk of being hit by rockets. But I am also told that the pilots like showing off to one another. When I asked a group of pilots over breakfast earlier that morning where they were going, they told me, 'To drop bombs on Afghanistan.' That's what they do. They eat eggs and have a coffee, fly over to Afghanistan and kill people, then come back and have a chicken sandwich for lunch.

On the tour we drive past a jet that has something 'top secret' underneath it. It just looks like a box but who knows what it is or what it can do. We know it is top secret is by the red rope around the entire plane and a soldier with a gun sitting in a jeep minding it. If you cross the red rope you get shot. No questions. That's it. If I wasn't curious about what was under that plane I certainly am now. The soldier in the jeep is reading a book to pass the time. What an odd way to spend the day. *How was your day?* Oh, I read a couple of chapters of Harry Potter and shot two unauthorised personnel who tried to take a peek at my jet.

The other amazing aircraft is one I hear but don't see. That night, as our next gig approaches, I hear this almighty roar of jet engines flying overhead, like what you would hear at the end of a runway when a plane goes overhead. But when I look up I see nothing. It's unnerving to hear this amazing blast and then look up into an empty sky. I thought that it might be a stealth bomber but that is *sooo* Gulf War I.

Our second show in 'nowhere' turns out to be the weird-est show of the whole tour. Well, for me it was anyway.

We're performing in this huge outdoor pavilion and everyone from the camp is invited. There are hundreds of people here but there are only 60 Australians, max. The reason this gig sticks out as being bad is because no one cares that we are here.

This camp is specifically for rest and recuperation. The soldiers have had entertainment coming out of their ears. They can go and do a few laps in the pool, or play ping-pong, or go shopping for televisions in the electrical goods store. The vast majority of the audience is US Defence, who don't seem particularly excited about watching a few entertainers from Australia they've never heard of.

The other twist on this gig tonight is that I'm told I'm not allowed to swear. The camp commander is a Baptist and doesn't fancy coarse language. He doesn't have a problem with 'thou shalt not kill', but saying the word 'shit' will send him into a tailspin. Never mind that he isn't coming to the show. It's just that's the way he likes it.

To me this is red rag to a bull. So I open up my act with a bit of ... 'Apparently, I'm not allowed to swear here? Well FUCK that! We're in a war zone, I can't think of a more appropriate forum for swearing. If I get shot I'm going to swear. If I'm hit I'll be straight in there. BANG! CUNT! I won't be polite about it. I'm not going to be bleeding while saying I'd hate to offend a lady with my poor vocabulary, I'll be straight in there.'

My opening gets a ripple of excitement from the audience. Though I must say it's mostly from the Australian corner, which doesn't constitute anywhere near the majority, so you can barely say I am winning over the 'crowd'. So I launch into my favourite trick. If you've stepped over the line in stand-up the best thing to do is to own it.

'Sorry, I wasn't allowed to swear. What are you going to do? Send me back to Australia? What a shame! I won't get to hang around in this shit hole.' Cheers from the Australians. Begrudging respect from the Americans.

Adrian, Alan, the McClymonts and the RAAF band give it their best, but when the gig ends everyone in the area goes back to what they were doing like the show never happened. It was the kind of gig that gives you all the thrills of performing in the middle of a Westfield shopping centre. *None.*

Next day, we are due to go to Basra to entertain the

British troops and give them a bit of Commonwealth love. Due to how England is doing in the Ashes, I can't wait! But the shows never happen. We are on standby but things start to get too hairy in Basra for us to go. I ask Lieutenant Colonel Greg what is meant by 'hairy'.

'Not safe,' he replies.

'Is there a major operation going on?' I ask.

He doesn't answer. He just passes me a look that tells me I would have to survive on the amount of information that would not alarm a 19-year-old girl from Grafton. *Right*.

The upside of this is that out of nowhere we have a spare day, but it is the kind of day that sort of drifts past. You know, one of those days you have when you're overseas and you know you should be making the most of it but watching a DVD, doing a crossword or your laundry seems like the most enticing thing to do. So I do all of the above, call home, catch up on a few emails and use the time to rest and get over my cold.

We're sitting around having afternoon tea when Brooke asks Lieutenant Colonel Greg, 'When are we going to Baghdad?'

We all burst into delirious laughter. Then I politely explain, 'You know when we were pirates? *That* was Baghdad.'

'Ooooh.' Then Brooke adds, 'Well, where are we going next?'

Lieutenant Colonel Greg answers, 'Afghanistan.'

The laughter stops.

9

TARIN KOWT
THURSDAY, 28 DECEMBER 2006

We are the first show to go and entertain the Australian troops in Afghanistan, which brings up a feeling of excitement and trepidation amongst all of us. Being part of a rotating roster of entertainers at a massive US airbase was one thing, but actually going out to the front line where soldiers really needed it is another.

Our first stop is Tarin Kowt in the Oruzgan province in southern Afghanistan, an amazing piece of country. The military base is in the middle of a bowl of mountains that are all higher than Mount Kosciusko, which is not saying much. Because of the mountainous terrain, our

Hercules has to do a steep dive into the bowl and land on a dirt strip.

We land with a thud – *I am getting used to this* – and dust flies up everywhere. We know we are somewhere serious because when we get off the plane we're instructed not to take off our flak jackets. On this arrival, there's no minibus with an armed driver to pick us up, instead there are several armoured personnel carriers that the Australians call Bushmasters. I know it makes them sound like a four-burner barbecue but I assure you they look imposing. All the Australian soldiers look focused and ready 'at the trigger', which fills the air with that extra bit of tension. We all get loaded like cattle up a ramp onto the back of the Bushmasters. There are no windows inside, so this is not going to be a scenic drive to the camp.

Once we get going, the man in charge of the Bushmaster informs me that each time they drive in and out of the base they take a different route. 'The Taliban are observing us so we try to keep them guessing by not establishing any routines.' *Note to self: try to be as unpredictable as possible on this leg of the trip.*

The camp is a walled compound within a walled compound. The walls are huge and made of earth packed inside hessian and wire, which is supposedly the best material for absorbing rocket blasts. Our accommodation area is also surrounded by concrete walls, to deflect rockets and decrease the chances of being hit by one. We are shown where the bomb shelter is located, so that we know how to make our way there in the event of an attack.

As I walk through the freezing cold to our accommodation I begin to see the differences in the soldiers stationed here. These soldiers don't really stop to give you a cheery wave like the ones we've become accustomed to in Iraq; I can only describe them as stressed. The soldiers are from the Australian First Reconstruction Task Force. They go out and try to win over the hearts and minds of the local Afghanis by building hospitals and schools and providing them with options. A large part of their job is providing security for the engineers who are doing this good work, because the Taliban take an active interest in not letting it happen.

Commander Jonathan, who is in charge of this camp, tells me that when they travel around to some of the villages in the local areas it's like stepping back to medieval times. A lot of villages have no electricity or sewerage. People just defecate in the streets.

'Make no mistake,' Commander Jonathan warns us, 'the Taliban are watching our every move. They are observing us right now trying to work out *their* next move. We had a rocket come into the camp last night, but don't worry, we've never had a rocket enter the camp two nights in a row, so I'm sure you'll be fine.' *Thanks for that. Now I feel perfectly safe. That is a bit too much information for a 19-year-old girl from Grafton.*

I notice a strange thing about the camp. I see a man in traditional Afghani dress walking towards the laundry and my first thought is, 'One's got in!' Later I find out though that some locals are allowed to work within the camp. Of course, no one has told me this. I also find out that they can't tell friend from foe. I'm no expert so I just have to take it on faith that this is all very sensible to someone somewhere.

While killing some time in the afternoon I come across a cricket pitch where three local boys are playing cricket. I am curious how Afghanis know how to play cricket. Then it suddenly dawns on me that Afghanistan is on the border of Pakistan, so why wouldn't they? There are no photos allowed in the camp at Tarin Kowt, security is too tight. But this is the only photo I will regret not taking: a picture of these boys playing cricket like any boys in a street in Australia, framed by soldiers doing pistol training against targets on a wall, and behind that, in the distance, huge snow-capped mountains. It's a photo I have in my head and, unfortunately, that's the only place it exists.

The smiles on the faces of these boys are inspiring. Not because they evoke hope, but because they remind me that people live here – they actually *live* here. To them, this big weird war is something they've always known. To them, Australia's military presence may just mean that they now have a decent pitch to play cricket. We play for a while. When we do chat it is limited because of the language barrier, but I do learn that they think Steve Waugh is great and that Ricky Ponting is shit. Looks like Ricky Ponting should get over here to try and win some hearts and minds.

There is an attitude in Afghanistan that the army has to make the locals like them if they are to succeed in their mission here. I find this refreshing compared to the attitude in Iraq, which seemed more to be: 'Why don't these ungrateful bastards appreciate us invading their country?' Having Afghanis in the camp is also some-what special for me because I get to play cricket with them instead of staring at them through wire. We don't talk about politics or the war. I just try to bowl them out and those ungrateful bastards hit me for six ...

The camp in Tarin Kowt is an Australian camp joined to a Dutch camp. Like all the other camps, the Australians mooch off another country for the dining facility and in this case it is the Dutch. To get to the Dutch camp you have to go through what is known as 'The Portal'. This is a double set of gates the size of a small doorway. The idea is, in the event of one of the camps being overrun, you seal one camp off from the other.

As soon as you climb through the portal the first thing you're struck by is that the Dutch are downhill from the Australians and living in mud. An Australian soldier tells me it's because the Dutch haven't put in any drainage systems yet, as they're too busy rooting. All the countries away on operations take great pleasure in whispering to you that the Dutch are the only army who are allowed to 'fraternise' on base. I just think it is funny that even when at war, the Dutch manage to do their best to get below sea level.

The fringe benefit of going to the Dutch dining facility is that it's the only time we get to eat non-American food. I can't really explain what Dutch food is like except that the vegetables aren't overcooked and the desserts are a little more exotic. I'm told that I can look forward to seeing the Dutch that evening at the show because they'll be half the crowd. Half the crowd will have English as a second language – these gigs are getting more and more interesting by the day.

When I walk back to my accommodation to freshen up before the show I find the atmosphere of the camp a little eerie. All the lights are out except for little dull red lamps that are positioned around the place so you can see where you're going. I walk past a hut with its door open. All I can see inside are the silhouettes of a couple of guys smoking while death metal quietly throbs away, filling up their patch of the camp with a pent-up energy; quite a contrast to the clear night sky in which you can see these huge beautiful mountains.

On the way to the gig I ask someone why all the lights are out. 'That's to minimise our chances of being hit by a rocket,' he says. And to think at pub gigs I used to worry about people throwing beer cans.

The show that night stands out as one of my favourites. (On reflection, it was the best show of the entire trip.) By the standard of gigs I've done around the place, this one should have been a shocker. First of all, it is outdoors. Comedians hate that. No atmosphere. Then there's the fact that it is about zero degrees with no heating. There are no chairs either, so the soldiers, all rugged up in their winter gear, have to huddle around the veranda area of the recreation common room that is acting as a stage. Then, of course, half the audience is Dutch. But there is something there that night which cancels out all these negatives. Everyone is full of a desire for it to be great. It is the first time they've had a show at this camp, so they are all going to have a great time no matter what.

As soon as the RAAF band fires up, the soldiers start dancing in their winter kit. Adrian and Alan each do their bit and it goes over the best I've seen yet. When I come out I want to do some stuff about this audience and the fact that we are on the front line. After chatting to the Australians I yell, 'Are there any Dutch in?' *Huge cheer.* 'I went to your camp through 'The Portal'. You should call it 'The Asshole', because you climb through a tiny hole and once you get inside you find yourself in mud.' *The Australians cheer derisively.* Sometimes it pays to keep it basic. 'Us Australians can laugh all we want, but the Dutch troops are allowed to *fraternise* on base. I must say to the Dutch, you are the most relaxed fighting force I have ever seen in my life.' *Much cheering from the Dutch. Much jealousy from the Australians.*

This gig is one of the weirdest gigs I've done in my life and I am loving it. I thought I would cap it off by pointing out just how silly the whole scenario was. 'Your camp commander made me feel welcome by reminding me that the Taliban are watching us all the time. Thanks for that. And then when I was walking around I asked why all the lights were turned off, and a guy told me it was to minimise our chances of being a target for rocket attacks. So then I come outside to do this gig for you tonight and what do you have? A SPOTLIGHT ON MY FUCKING HEAD!' *The place erupts.* I know when to leave the stage. Thank you. Goodnight. I'm outta there.

The McClymonts come on and light up the stage in their special way. Afterwards, soldiers line up for ages to get a photo. Everyone seems to be quite buoyant after the show, even so, in less than an hour we're all in bed because it's an early start the next day.

At breakfast, Alan tells me a lovely story. 'After the show, I was having a cup of tea with a hard-looking bloke. He said that he had such a great time. It was the first time he has laughed, or even smiled, in months. And while he's telling me this, tears start streaming down his face. Not in a self-conscious way. It was just the way it was.'

For a comedian who originally came to this war zone 'to have a look', I was now getting a bit more than I bargained for.

10

KANDAHAR
FRIDAY, 29 DECEMBER 2006

We fly out of Tarin Kowt later that morning with the warm glow of a job well done. After a three-hour flight we arrive in another big NATO base in Kandahar.

Here, there is none of this coalition-of-the willing bullshit. Everyone is here. The camp has a truly international flavour. Apart from the Americans and Australians I've become accustomed to seeing, there are also Canadians, New Zealanders, and people I first thought were British but turn out to be Romanians with a similar uniform. You know who they are when they're dressed in their physical training (PT) gear, because they wear body tights that aren't very macho. There is a Russian massage parlour too with a big sign out the front that says: 'strictly non-sexual only'; and a Canadian doughnut house which has a sign out the front that says: 'strictly non-sexual only'. Okay, they didn't, but it would have been funny if they did.

When we get to the Australian corner, we are welcomed by Commander Cameron who wants to give us a little 'brief'. We have had to sit through quite a few briefs by now on this trip, but this was the most opposite-of-brief 'briefs' we've experienced so far. This guy over-explains everything. At one stage he says, 'We have a lot of facilities here that you should feel free to use. We've got the internet where you can check your Hotmail, or Yahoo, or Gmail, or any number of email providers, because it is part of the World Wide Web which connects computers together around the world as part of the information superhighway.' *WE KNOW WHAT THE INTERNET IS!*

Then on the way in to lunch Commander Cameron says to us, 'Now make sure you wash your hands with anti-bacterial soap because it gets rid of the bacteria on your hands and that will stop you getting a bacterial infection when ...' *I LEARNT THAT WHEN I WAS FIVE!*

That night, after a barbecue, we do a small gig just for the Australians. Commander Cameron has told me I can say what I want, just don't use the C word. 'Okay,' I reply.

I open up the act by saying, 'Commander Cameron told me I could say what I wanted so long as I don't say *cunt*. But if I get shot that's what I am going to say!' *Everyone's laughing. I'm off to a good start.* This is where I decide to dig in further with my worst-case-scenario-I'll-get-sent-home-to-Australia attitude.

'Commander Cameron likes to *over-explain* things, doesn't he? This morning he spent an hour explaining to me what a bed was: You see, this is a *bed*. What you do is lie on it horizontally, shut your eyes and wait for this other-worldly feeling that you're not quite there. That's called *sleep*, but don't worry, it will wear off in eight to nine hours at which point you just open your eyes and it's a brand new day. See what we're in now, it's called *day*. See how the sun is up in the air ... Now *air,* that's important. You've got to breathe that in and out. Not once! Constantly. Otherwise you will die, which is a bit like being asleep, which we discussed earlier, but you never wake up. Any questions?' *The crowd is on my wavelength.* I think they have sat through a lot more boring briefs than I have.

Commander Cameron redeems himself afterwards by doing the good Aussie thing and wearing the joke. He says, 'I thought I told you not to say the C word. It was pretty funny though. Do you want me to explain why? It only takes an hour.'

Next day, I take a wander around the camp. We are shown one of the Chinooks that Australia uses in Afghanistan. Graham, who had previously seen me do a gig in Townsville, says that we're allowed to take photos but only up close and inside the Chinook. Apparently, the security concern on an airstrip is not about what helicopters you've got, it's how many helicopters you've got and where they are sitting. These helicopters have two large rotors of about the same size and they are capable of transporting a jeep. Graham is a couple of years younger than I am and, like me, comes from country New South Wales. He is a helicopter pilot in a war; I am a man who says swear words into a microphone. There is a little moment of reflection there.

That afternoon was probably the most scared I felt during the whole trip. Nothing really happened except, as usual, in my imagination. I'm lying in bed at the barracks reading *Flags of Our Fathers*. (Did I mention that I'm a slow reader?) I hear the sound of small arms fire and an interchange with a machinegun. I immediately think it might have been the sound of someone dying; the sound of people fighting for their lives. My heart starts thumping as my imagination ups the ante ...

Maybe it's the sound of an attack on the camp. Maybe they're coming towards me. What will I do? The rest of the group is elsewhere. I am essentially on my own. What will I do if the camp gets overrun and I'm out here alone in the barracks while everyone else has hunkered down, safe and defended? I am unarmed. I don't have a mobile phone, I can't ring anyone.

As all these thoughts run through me in a split second and I start to really get a bit worked up, the door opens and Lieutenant Colonel Greg walks in with a towel wrapped around him. 'Are you all right, Tom?'

'Listen. I can hear the sound of gunfire. Is that from outside the wire?' I ask, feeling a bit silly.

'It's *probably* just a firing range,' he says.

Not, it *is* a firing range, but, *probably*. I'm not sure what this kind of 'probably' means. He might have meant it in the same way as 'it's *probably* time for lunch', but he could have meant it in the way an ANZAC at Gallipoli might have said, 'We are probably on the wrong beach.' Either way, the tension is dispersed and I return to reading about the misery that was the battle for Iwo Jima.

Saddam Hussein was hanged today. There were no celebrations. No songs or streamers. I don't even remember who it was that told me. It was said with all the excitement of a cricket score. I suppose that means that the war is over ... *Why do I get the feeling that this will change nothing?*

The show that night is held out in the main camp and everyone is invited. It is the most international audience that we've had to date, so I take my standard approach: if in doubt, make sure you offend everybody.

'Are there any Americans in? Thanks for supporting Australia's war against Iraq.' *This was turning into an old standard.* 'Are there any Australians in? Thanks for supporting New Zealand's war against Iraq.' *Too easy.* 'Are there any Canadians in? I love Canada. It's my favourite part of America.' *Cheap, but effective.* 'Are there any English in? I'm glad that you're not like your cricket team. Otherwise, after winning Basra, nine months later you would just give it back!' *I knew I'd get that line out some time.* 'Are there any Dutch here? No? Oh that's because they're all too busy fucking.' *A bit blue but it worked.* 'Are there any Romanians in? I like your PT gear. What are you training for? Being gay?' *And finally, an old favourite.* 'Are there any TCNs in? No? That's because they're too busy cleaning up all your shit for two dollars a day.'

It is like the United Nations of insults. *Too much fun.*

After the show, Lieutenant Colonel Greg tells me to get some sleep as we're getting up early tomorrow to fly to another country that I can't talk about. I get to be 'nowhere' again! Wooooooo ... noooooooowhere! *I really have to stop doing this.*

11

SECRET COUNTRY NO. 3
SUNDAY, 31 DECEMBER 2006

While we wait for the Hercules to come and pick us up I sit in the strangest departure lounge. The building is known as the TLS or Taliban's Last Stand. I remember seeing this building in the news at the end of 2001. This was where the last Taliban fighters in Kandahar fell back before they fought to the death. As I'm sitting here watching the other members of our merry group reading magazines or wrestling with a Coke machine that doesn't want to spit out the right change, I can't help noticing the amazing number of bullet holes in the wall. For the Americans it represented victory or justice, but you can't ignore the confronting truth that a lot of people died in this room – this room full of people drinking coffee and doing crosswords. It's easy to call the Taliban fanatics, but it's harder to think that they really believed in what they were doing. I can't think of anything I believe in strong enough that's worth dying for. Maybe that's why I point at things and make jokes for a living.

We arrive in another 'nowhere'. What is it with these secret countries and their level of comfort? We're at another airbase and I've been told that the air force likes the finer things in life. There's an old joke, though I hadn't heard it: *Why doesn't the air force have three-star generals? In the air force it's five stars or nothing.* This place has everything we have come to expect at an airbase, with a little bit more – *separate rooms!*

Oh my god, we all have our own rooms for the first time in ages! On this leg, Alan's snoring can keep itself company. Everyone is so excited about the simple pleasure of having a tiny piece of privacy. I'm just excited about the thought of having an afternoon nap that lasts longer than ten minutes. So we all hurry off and disappear into our rooms – in my case, for quite some time. Tonight's gig is going to be special. It's New Year's Eve.

But here's the twist, in this country alcohol is forbidden. We are going to spend New Year's Eve getting trashed on tea and biscuits! It's going to be the first New Year's that I'll be able to remember what has happened since I was 16. *Or was it 15?*

Our gig is on an outdoor stage, which is fine because this secret country is not that cold. The audience is about eighty people made up of Australians, Canadians, British and a couple of New Zealanders. If anything, they are a bit subdued. When I'm not on stage, I sit in the audience and really take in everyone's performances. I know that before long these shows will be a distant memory.

Time for the count down. 10! 9! 8! 7! 6! 5! 4! 3! 2! 1! Happy New Year! Yay! Everyone kisses each other to welcome in the new year, which has a whole new spin on it when you're sober. Everyone still seems pretty excited nonetheless. We all have one thing in common: we are celebrating the new year in a country we officially aren't in. So when we return home and anyone asks, 'Where were you on New Year's Eve?' we can answer, literally, 'Nowhere.' And they'll say, 'Yeah, I didn't do much either. It's over-rated as a night out.'

After the gig, Brooke, Sam, Molly and I are too excited

to go to bed and it seems pretty lame to be in bed just after midnight. So here's what we do. We go to the cafeteria and drink tea, eat cakes and talk shit, which involves Brooke telling embarrassing stories about herself and us laughing too much. One story involves her going out on a date and experimenting with wearing a wig only to end up dragging her feet home with the wig limp and lifeless in her hand. Then we run outside and play basketball with a flat ball. Not many points are scored. We just mostly collapse on each other and laugh too hard at how unco we are. Then Molly yells, 'What's next?' And we run onto a hockey field where we play hockey, which mostly involves Sam getting too competitive and the rest of us trying to belt the stick out of her hands. Then we retire to my room where I teach them all how to play poker.

I take the girls through the order of hands starting with the Royal Flush and working my way down. I give them the standard line that poker is a game of perceived skill, but really it relies on luck and anyone can win, even a beginner. We use matches for chips, it's five dollars in and I pull out my 'Iraq's Most Wanted' playing cards where Saddam Hussein is the ace of spades. We play and laugh into the wee hours and you'd never guess what happens, I win all their money – fifteen dollars worth.

By now, we are absolutely exhausted. I have never laughed so hard in my life. It's the kind of fun you had when you were a kid and your parents had friends over and so the kids were allowed to stay up later than usual. I don't know whether it was being sober, the bonhomie or the sugar rush, but the next morning I wake up refreshed and facing a new year without a hangover. It's an amazing feeling. I know it sounds like one of those 'first day of the rest of my life' scenarios and that I've turned over a new leaf, but I can assure you that leaf has since been turned back over and over several times.

12

PLAYING POKER WITH THE SAS
SOMEWHERE IN THE MIDDLE EAST

There's one part of my trip so far I have left out — it's when I meet the SAS. I wanted to save this highlight of my trip for the end. Of course, I can't tell you where it was or when it was because — well — they're the SAS.

———

At one gig the SAS are there. I recognise them straight-away because they have big long beards, which they grow to blend in with the locals. So when I spot them in the crowd, I say, 'If you guys want to blend in with the locals, why don't you just fuck a goat?' Now I know that this is not particularly clever and it certainly isn't culturally sensitive, but sometimes on stage you do what you've got to do. I get nothing. No response. I try to make light of it and engage them some other way, but they aren't having a bar of it.

After the gig, one of them approaches me and says in a flat tone, 'The reason we weren't talking to you on stage is because we're the SAS. No one's supposed to know we're here yet, but they do now because you talked to us through a microphone that is connected to speakers which can be heard outside the camp.' *There's a long pause.* His clear blue eyes are drilling a hole in my head. 'But don't worry about that. The enemy would have soon known that we were here anyway when their friends start turning up dead.'

He just stares at me. Am I supposed to laugh? Who is this guy?

'Do you want a beer?' he asks.

Now at this stage I hadn't had a drink for a long while. So I say, 'Yes!'

'All right,' he continues. 'Well, why don't you come back to our secret headquarters and have a few beers, but just keep that on the QT. I don't want anyone around here knowing that we've got alcohol.' *Okay.* Now, when the SAS tell you to keep a secret, you take that shit seriously.

This guy with a beard but without a name then puts me in a four-wheel drive with a bag over my head because he doesn't want me knowing where he's taking me. I distinctly remember sitting there thinking, 'I really, *really*, *REALLY* have to learn to say no. I'm just too fucking agreeable.'

So after a short drive (which makes me think that the bag on my head is a joke) we arrive at their secret headquarters. The bag comes off to reveal it's a really small area within a larger camp made up of three small demountables. I'm allowed into only one of them. In the dark of night it's hard to see, but I'm told to look out for ditches that the SAS are in the middle of digging. Apparently they've only just moved in and are still setting up. The inside of the small demountable is spartan. Nothing seems to give away that I'm in a top-secret headquarters of an elite fighting force. Most of the equipment lying around resembles camping gear. I could easily be in a field office of the National Parks and Wildlife except these bearded men are clearly not bushwalkers.

Here we are, about 12 of us sitting around a big table. These guys look imposing with their beards. They are all wearing mismatched plain clothes with nothing on them that clearly defines them as military except for their demeanour. None of them smoke because they need every scrap of fitness for combat operations. They're not as physically big as you would think either, but their bodies have a lean efficiency that enables them to survive on long-range missions that other countries' forces don't even attempt to make. To say they come with a reputation is an understatement. I am awestruck.

They hand me a can of Tiger beer. It goes down easy and out comes another. Despite the beers on offer, the conversation is pretty stilted at first because everything is a secret. I ask all these questions.

'What did you do today?'

Nothing.

'Have you been on any missions?'

Nothing.

'Are you planning any missions?'

Nothing.

'Have you killed anyone?'

Nothing.

'What's that map on the wall?'

'Don't look at that!' comes the response. They want to turn the attention on to me.

'What do you do for fun back home?' they ask.

'Well, I like to play poker,' I reply.

With that, out come two decks of cards, chips, more beers and everyone is twenty dollars in. *This is great! I'm playing poker with the SAS!* And then I think what am I doing? This is *the* SAS. They sneak into countries where they don't belong. They've been trained to withstand interrogation and torture. Their whole lives are a secret and I'm going to try and beat them in a game of bluff?

It turns out that only a few of them are good at poker. Some have no idea what's going on. They establish a rule that when you are betting you throw your chips high in the air with the intention of them landing on the table. If a chip rolls off the table, it's not counted and goes back in the pot.

Several guys go 'all in' with the first round of betting. Unsurprisingly, it seems one trait they all have in common is risk-taking behaviour. Guys are losing their money and buying back in rapidly. *I might win a few US dollars tonight!*

Now that we're playing, the stories start to flow. Gus, who seems to be the one in charge, tends to hold the floor most easily. He starts up with, 'Once, when I was meeting with a group of warlords ...' *Everyone goes quiet.*

'It was a Thursday, which around here we call man-love night. All the local men get dressed up with eye-liner and make-up. The women stay home and the men go out and hold hands together.' He says this with a smirk. 'So I'm chatting to the tribal leader, trying to find out what's going on in the local area. He has a boy sitting next to him looking at him with doey eyes and I think, "That's a bit suss". At which point I feel someone leaning on my side and look around and there's another boy looking up lovingly at me. The tribal leader looks at me as if to say, "What do you reckon?" And at this point I decide to leave because there's only so much I'll do for my country. I love Australia but not that much!' *Everyone laughs.*

The conversation then turns to how much they hate the regular Army, all the rules and the soldiers that follow them blindly. Chris, the guy that brought me to their HQ, chimes in with a story.

'When we first got here, the camp was being set up by the Army. We had gone off on an operation that had lasted about two months and when we came back to base we were filthy. You know? You've been living off the land, you haven't had a shower because you don't want your smell to give your position away, your hair is all matted up and you really, really fuckin' stink and all you want is a nice hot shower. So we get back to base and these stupid army cunts have been there for two months and they haven't even connected the hot water. Me and Carl are just there under the cold shower yelling at the top of our lungs, YOU FUCKIN' ARMY CUNTS! CAN'T EVEN CONNECT A FUCKIN' TAP.'

We're laughing and having a great time and as the stories flow so did the beers. We're all getting a bit loose. The betting is becoming sillier and sillier and then, lo and behold, I am up $120. Now, the trick to winning poker is that when you're ahead, you leave. *Problem is, I can't leave. I don't know where I am!*

And every time I attempt to leave Gus says, 'Do you want another beer?'

And I say, 'I don't want another beer.'

And he'd yell, 'Come on! When can you say you got pissed in a war zone?'

I can't argue with that.

When the night finally wraps up I am about $30 dollars up, which is not too bad. Carl, one of the furriest of the men, offers me a lift back to where I'm staying. I suppose you can't get done for drink-driving in a war zone, there are bigger fish to fry. When I jump into the ute he says in a leading fashion, 'Do you like the ute?'

'Yeah, I suppose.'

'It costs about $250,000.' It is then that I notice the glass is about an inch thick, and all the doors are heavily reinforced and there are a few extra levers other than the gearstick.

'But it looks like a normal ute,' I say.

He fixes me a cheeky gaze, 'Exactly!' With that we're off to my accommodation.

No bag on my head this time. I'm too drunk to know where I am anyway. On the way back Carl confides to me, 'You know we get counselling here if we want it but we're all pretty strong mentally. That's why they chose us. In training they beat you up with phone books and all kinds of stuff I won't bother you with and you do see some pretty horrific shit. But when you're out there and the adrenaline is pumping, you've got bullets whizzing all round you, you know you might die ... I gotta say, it's the best job in the world. I absolutely love it.'

When I get to my room, Lieutenant Colonel Greg asks me if I had a good night. 'I'm going straight to bed!' I blurt out in the same manner a teenager does to avoid their parents for fear of them smelling their breath.

I see them at a nearby market the next day. They must have the day off. They are the only ones cruising around the market speaking to the locals in their native tongue. Gus tells me in a sheepish way that they all must have turned into a light touch while on operations. They're all quite hungover. I am on the same page.

Carl, the furry-faced fellow, invites me over to have tea and a chat with a local man. We squat and the two of them chat. My furry-faced friend offers to buy me a pirated DVD. I ask him to buy me his favourite war film. He gives me a copy of *The Beast*. I hadn't heard of it.

'Watch it and you'll know what all this rubbish is about,' he says. (I end up watching it when I get back home to Australia. Some parts of it are so arresting that I have to put the DVD on pause for a breather.)

They all come to our next show. I now know better and avoid making any goat-fucking jokes. After the gig I thank them all for a great night. I mention, as a gesture, that I would love to get a photo of us together, but obviously I can't for security reasons. At that, my furry friend says, 'Yes you can. Why not? Don't worry about it.' We all huddle in and 1, 2, 3, click.

As Gus hands me back the camera, he says, 'If that photo ends up on the internet I'll shoot you in the fucking head.' They all laugh, a bit too hard, and for a bit too long. To this day I still don't know if they were joking or not.

13

THE BOAT
MONDAY, 1 JANUARY 2007

Our last show is on the deck of the HMAS *Warramunga*.
I'm told that it is a ship. Don't call it a boat. The navy
hates that.

To get to the ship we have to leave the Australian base
and enter Secret Country No. 3, so we have to have our
diplomatic passports ready. We are told that when we go
through the inspection area we will have to get out of
the bus, line up with our passports ready and be polite.

After what seems like ages, we're finally given the heads
up. The customs officials, or whoever they are, don't

like us much. We are told to get off the bus in a line. We stand there while they go through our passports, staring at us imposingly with their machine-guns at their hip. Australians don't take this well. We think we're laid back, but we're not. Here are some government officials giving us a good lookover because we invaded a neighbouring country and they don't even want us there. Instead of showing any empathy all we can think is: 'They were a bit full-on!'

On the HMAS *Warramunga* we meet the captain, who takes us to his 'quite plush' quarters and offers us a beer. *There goes my New Year's resolution!* The Navy know what they're doing! He informs us that this is the only ship that Australia has in the Gulf and it is here to help protect the oil output of Iraq, which apparently accounts for about 90 per cent of the country's GDP. When tankers from around the world dock at Iraq's oil platforms they are boarded and accompanied by armed US soldiers who stand beside the ship's captain as they dock. Think about that next time you feel a bit of pressure when a stranger takes a particular interest in your ability to parallel park in a tight spot.

I get a tour around the deck and a crew member shows me one of the machine-guns. After giving me all of its specs and the damage it could do, he adds, 'So far, we haven't had to use it and I hope we never do.' This is a fully armed ship in the middle of a war zone and it hasn't fired one single shot! Think about that next time you see Lisa McCune pumping out rounds into some drug-smuggler's boat on *Sea Patrol*. *Yeah, right!*

Our last show, on the deck of the *Warramunga*, takes place on a beautiful, Middle Eastern winter's day with a big, clear, blue sky. We're all in good spirits because we know we'll be going home soon. All the crew is gathered on deck to watch. I feel like Cher in the film clip 'If I Could Turn Back Time'.

I start the show on the typical front foot. 'Thank you for inviting me on to your BOAT! I know, I know, it's a ship.' *Jeers and cheers.* The ship behind us is French, so, deciding that they can hear me through the speakers I start yelling at them in bad schoolboy French. '*Bonjour! Où est les toilettes? Vous êtes petits cochons!*' Which approximately means you are little pigs. 'Nice BOAT!' *That'll show 'em.* Towards the end of the show the RAAF band play a song and the McClymonts, Alan and Adrian decide to join in. So I play tambourine. Adrian starts dancing with one of the ship's crew, then one of the female crew members jumps up and starts dancing with me. I turn my back to the audience to pretend I am making out with her, but this lady sailor's arms are quite strong and she forces my head towards hers and gives me a big pash! I suppose this woman had been at sea for a while and was a bit toey.

After the show everyone on the ship invites us down to their respective bars. I feel like I'm on a pub crawl beneath the decks of a boat – sorry, ship. There's the able seaman's bar, the petty officer's bar and on and on it goes. They're all a bit keen to squeeze another couple of Crown Lagers into me and I am starting to get a little loose.

Part of my foggy memories of that lost afternoon include a sailor showing me video footage of his R&R time with a Russian prostitute. *Thanks for that, mate.* I also remember trying really hard to act sober on our way back home to the secret country where no one is allowed to drink. When I was politely standing in line for the customs official, I think I was swaying a bit. I didn't get into trouble. Maybe it was because I said, 'thank you' about ten times after he approved my passport. It would have been terrible to stumble at the last step.

When I tell people about my trip, they ask me two things: Were you ever scared? And what did you get paid? I know that sounds rude, but as a comedian everyone wants to know what you're paid. Well, the answer in this case is not much. You get a small daily allowance to compensate for your time away and you get one day to go shopping in Dubai. If having one day of shopping in Dubai sounds exciting, let me tell you it isn't. I learnt something on this last day of the trip though. The army is really good at organising wars but not very good at organising shopping trips. There were about 40 of us going out at one time with one mobile phone and no passports. When you're in another country and you don't have your passport you can't afford to get lost. The mobile phone kept us tied together and we weren't allowed to separate for security reasons anyway. I felt like I did about five laps of the city and all I could find was one vaguely nice wallet and a pair of Diesel runners for the same price they would have been in Australia. It was like a death march for bargains.

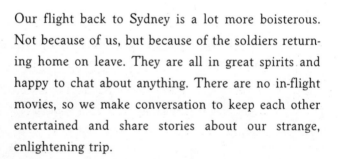

14

HOMEWARD
WEDNESDAY, 3 JANUARY 2007

Our flight back to Sydney is a lot more boisterous. Not because of us, but because of the soldiers returning home on leave. They are all in great spirits and happy to chat about anything. There are no in-flight movies, so we make conversation to keep each other entertained and share stories about our strange, enlightening trip.

When we arrive at Sydney Airport we say our awkward farewells to each other. We know it will be a long while before we see each other again − if at all − and it will never be under these circumstances. It was definitely a once-in-a-lifetime experience. I say goodbye to the band, and kiss Brooke, Sam, Molly and Toni farewell. I shake Alan's hand, and I ask Adrian, 'How's your *moom*?' to which he replies, 'Delightful!' I say thanks to Lieutenant Colonel Greg and Warrant Officer Andrew for looking after us undisciplined civilians and that is that. Then I skip off to catch my flight to Melbourne.

My girlfriend Ellie picks me up at the airport. I feel flat and lifeless.

'How was your trip?' she asks, enthused.

'Good,' is all I can manage.

'What was it like?'

'Interesting.' I have to apologise. 'I'm sorry. It was amazing. I don't know where to start. Just let me tell you in bits and pieces over the next couple of days and weeks. Here's a piece of marble from Saddam's palace. I'm sorry I didn't get you any duty free.' And then I ask, 'Did you miss me?'

In her typical understated way, Ellie replies, 'A little bit. You sound tired. Why don't you rest?'

She did miss me. A couple of days later, Ellie, the girl who told me she wasn't the marrying type, proposed to me. Nothing like the threat of death in a war zone to force a result.

A bit of a rule in stand-up comedy is that when you're making up material you should try to think of things that everybody can relate to. That's why a lot of comedians talk about funny ads on television, or a weird sign they've seen, or about relationships. After what I had experienced on tour, all that sounded so boring. Then again, talking about wars in countries that people have never been to, how is anyone going to relate to that?

A few nights after I get back I go to one of my favourite comedy venues to do a short spot. I get on stage and I just say, 'I did some gigs in Iraq.' Everyone immediately stops talking and stares towards the stage. You could hear a pin drop. 'I did! I went over there to entertain the troops.' This is a hip inner-city venue. The majority of Australians don't agree with the war, but absolutely no one agrees with it here. I continue.

'I know that some of you think that by going over there it means I support the war, but I want to point out that I didn't just go there to do comedy ...' *I draw them in* ... 'I went there to kill civilians.' *The crowd erupts.* They get my dry sense of humour here. They look at me with faces that say, 'and then what?' So I start to relate my travels to them. *They laugh. They listen.* The comedians come in from the other bar to see what I'm up to. When I lose my way I say, 'Are there any questions?' I'm on stage for over half an hour but the questions never run out. *What was it like? Were you scared? What did you get paid?* And on and on it goes. Just as I'm about to finally leave the stage someone yells out, 'How long were you over there for?'

I count up the days in my head. 'Two weeks.' I answer.

Two weeks? Is that it? Even as I say it I can't believe it. I usually don't fit that much excitement into a whole year. It was not a long trip, but I can honestly say it was the best two weeks of my life.